To Regina —
Breathe, smile and Pres
Always look within and
Find your inner-Peace

Mastering Success

Jose Incer

© 2012 by Jose Incer
All rights reserved. No part of this book may be reproduced, stored in a retrieval system or transmitted in any form or by any means without the prior written permission of the publishers, except by a reviewer who may quote brief passages in a review to be printed or electronically distribute in a newspaper, magazine, journal, website, or blog.

Cover design by Jose Incer
Cover photo from iStockphoto

ISBN 978-0-9885288-0-2 (paper)
ISBN 978-0-9885288-1-9 (digital)

This book is a reference work based on research by the author. The opinion express herein are not necessary those of or endorse by the Publisher.

Printed in the United State of America

I would like to express my eternal gratitude to my wife Deirdre Tannian and my mother Veronica Gutierrez; they are the pillars of strength that keep me going through all ups and downs of life.

To my professors Flavio S. Campos and Santiago Aranegui who have helped me so much. If you see any wisdom or truth in me, it is a glance of their essence.

To my colleagues Guillermo Leon and Miguel A. Gonzalez for all their support and understanding.

A special thanks to Chrissie Tannian for her assistance in editing of my book.

And to all my clients; with their unique life experiences they help me grow and expand my horizon.
My clients are my teachers.

"This is the ultimate fact: Thoughts become Beliefs, Beliefs become Energy, Energy becomes Action, Action becomes Manifestation."
- Jose Incer

Contents

Forewords By Hazel Blanco, Ph.D. xiii
A Note From Guillermo Leon C Ht xix
Introduction... xxiii

Part One: Watch Out For That First Step

1. The Power Of Listening..1
2. You Are What You Believe 9
3. Take Actions..17

Part Two: You Have All The Answers

4. Understanding 25
5. Acceptance 33
6. Forgiveness 41

Part Three: Who Is That In The Mirror?

7. Our Thoughts 49
8. Our Words 57
9. Our Behaviour 65

Part Four: Manifesting Your Goals

10. Imagination..73
11. Visualization...81
12. Meditation 89

Part Five: It Is All Around Us

13. Energy..97
14. Frequency...105
16. Manifestation 113

Part Six: The Truth And Nothing But The Truth

17. The Seven Universal Laws...121
18. The Cycle Of Life..133
19. Light At The End Of The Tunnel 143

Part Seven: Conclusion

20. Keep Moving Forward...151
21. Share the knowledge..155

Forewords By Hazel Blanco Ph.D.

Ever since ancient Greece a separation has been made between mind and body, this powerful paradigm has had an incredible amount of influence throughout history, even in our current era; traditional medicine is characterized by making this separation a common practice every day in doctor's offices, clinics, hospitals and research laboratories.

With this in mind, for a long period it was thought that our capacity for change was very little, that our personality, behaviours and habits were formed in our childhood and from this point on there was not much that could be changed, hence the saying *"This is how I am and this is how I am going to die."* Unfortunately this philosophy serves as a justification for the lifestyle so many people live, even today.

However, in the late 1960's and early 1970's neuroscientists made a series of dramatic discoveries, the research demonstrated that the human brain is moldable. Our brain constantly changes with each activity that we do. Furthermore, a number of scientists have demonstrated that during the process of thinking, learning and executing certain activities turns "On" or turns "Off" our genes, therefore shaping our brain anatomy and consequently our behaviour, our body chemistry and the way in which the cells divide.

We are in the midst of a paradigmatic revolution in the way we view the connection between the mind and body and the mind and the brain. Today there is a valid notion that every human being is an integration. What affects the mind is going to affect the body and vice versa, the separation between physical health and mental health is fiction, and even the WHO (World Health Organization) maintains that the majority of physical and mental illnesses influence one another, through psychological, biological and social factors.

Forewords by Hazel Blanco Ph.D.

This paradigmatic revolution is great news for the people and therapists who work day after day contributing toward the quality of life that people desire. We are able to accomplish this through the growth and improvements that every person experiences, as we continue to look for the physical, mental and spiritual development. From this point of view every therapist is also a neuroscientist.

When Jose told me that he had written a book I asked him about the topic. He responded that it was about personal, physical and emotional growth, but he immediately stated "I don't want to call it a self-help book." After reading it, I realized that it is a book written by a person who has given himself the task to study, learn and evolve as an individual. He has the reins of his life in his own hands.

With this knowledge he also has taken the decision to become a leader and a shining light to illuminate the path of those who choose to improve their lives. There is a famous quote by Nelson Mandela, that states *"Our deepest fear is not that we are inadequate. Our deepest fear is that we are powerful beyond measure. It is our light, not our darkness that most frightens us. We ask ourselves, Who am I to be brilliant, gorgeous, talented, fabulous? Actually, who are you not to be?"* and in this book, Jose shows us a path of light to become beings full of light.

This book is more a philosophy of life. Is a choice on how to obtain personal freedom, to acquire the benefits of a full and fruitful life, to become not a spectator but the main actor in our life. There is a very clear message that this book communicates: *"To always be aware that the only one responsible for my life is myself, even if I want to justify my actions by projecting the blame to others,"* that is the first step to be taken.

It is all about having a choice on how I'm going to build the life that I want, a choice not to live in fear but rather having the courage to take chances. There are people who say they fear the future, I would say to them that the future can be seen now, most people act surprised even shocked when I make this statement, I explain to them that if they want to know how their future will be, all they have to do is just look at their lives in the present, because the decisions taken or not taken in the present, will be what they will have in the future, the same way that the present is what they did or did not do in my past.

That is the work of Jose in this book, a philosophy on life to grow and evolve as a person, as a human being but in an integrative way: physical, emotional, mental, social and spiritual.

A few years ago I read a quote that is attributed to Democritus *"Men ask in their prayers for health from the gods, but do not know that the power to attain this lies in themselves,"* and definitely, with this book, that is the great contribution that Jose passes down to all of us. The improvement in the quality of life, to become a light and to shine.

A Note From Guillermo Leon C Ht.

Sometimes people hold on to a belief system with the assumption that this same belief system might make them somehow unique; instead they end up being a victim of this system. Believe it or not, about five years ago I was one of these victims. My mind embarked in the relentless pursuit to become unique. I created an illusion by trying to resolve all my problems by seeking revenge on all my "enemies." It took me sometime to discover and understand that the battle was not with the "outside world," the real battle was raging within me, with my own thoughts and actions.

You may ask what led to the realization to make such a profound statement like the one above? It all started in the same classroom where Jose Incer and I met. Our life journey brought us to this special place where we started to acquire some of the answers we were searching for; answers that allowed us to learn and understand how to avoid the causes of negative outcomes but more importantly to pave the way to a successful life. Through the course of time we have expanded our horizons by spending countless hours studying and researching a wide spectrum of knowledge. This is how I discovered some of the qualities that Jose Incer possessed. His special inquisitive nature and his dramatic outlook drives not only his determination to succeed but also made it possible for me to understand that he will not stop until he does great things for humanity.

His work **Mastering Success** is not only the result of unceasing careful research and interpretation but also the result of his ability to combine his own life experiences on a case by case basis. It is this constant effort, dedication and will that allow him to move forward.

This book is about taking control of your belief system with a process that is simple, far simpler that most people realize. This is not an elaborate process of complicated theories and

A Note From Guillermo Leon

concepts explaining why people's lives are unbalanced. Instead, it is the simple road to understand the process between *creating something* and *making something up*. In other words the way we perceive and interpret the world around us. It a reminder that sadness, anxiety or low self esteem are all complicated illusions made up in our minds.

Sometimes people hold back because they think that their problems are going to be with them forever. The good news is that it is possible to enjoy freedom from most of our problems. How do you do this? When you think differently for the better, then you act differently for the better.

Mastering Success is a behavioral and philosophical guide with esoteric components that demonstrate a simple way for anyone to improve his or her life. It is a source to find some of the answers to materialize our dreams, to find the path to freedom and control our own destiny.

Introduction

Mastering Success

More and more people are seeking to achieve a higher level of consciousness and self-empowerment; one in which they manage their own destiny by unleashing their inner-strength and resources. This dynamic process begins with the understanding that we hold the key to all our achievements and successes, by the same token it is essential to realize that we also hold the dagger of failure, if we choose to.

The truth is that we are living in exciting times; we are in the midst of a great shift in consciousness. Slowly, we are realizing that we carry all the answers with us; this allows us to recognize that we can be at peace even in the most stressful environment or be miserable in the most pleasant place imaginable; it is all up to us, and that is empowering.

It is always with great joy that I watch a client and fellow human being continue to move forward in her/his personal, professional and spiritual life; all of us are here in this world on a special mission, to learn and evolve. It is for this reason that I decided to write this book. It is my wish that the knowledge on these pages will help you achieve a better life.

You have the right to live a balanced, productive, and successful life. Just like everyone else, you have goals that you want to achieve; I want to help you acquire them; whatever you need or desire can be yours. Let me assure you that you can attain all your goals if you grasp the understanding to know what to do and how to do it. By writing this book, all I'm doing is sharing information of things you might have sensed or felt in the past but could not quite understand it. So it is up to you to accept or reject any of the principles and concepts presented here. Always do your best to keep an open mind and remember that knowledge is essential for personal and collective growth.

You might not be aware but every event you encounter in your

Introduction

daily life has a beginning in the deepest level of your mind; you are responsible for every single experience you encounter. It's true, what you believe to be reality, is no more than a collection of perceptions, programs, and opinions that you have about yourself and the world around you.

With this book you will learn practical techniques for meditation, visualization, self hypnosis, developing your intuition, and bringing energy and healing to your life. Use your judgment in performing these techniques; practice the exercises you feel comfortable with and disregard the others. All the exercises are simple, easy, and fast. Of course, these exercises requires an effort of the will and you may not be entirely successful at first, but keep practicing and you will succeed. I have worked with many clients from all walks of life, we utilize these same simple exercises I describe in this book to successfully heal numerous conditions and to achieve their personal, professional, and spiritual goals. Sometimes the change might be pretty small but if you maintain that change over a period of time you eventually will get closer to you goals and away from the place where you no longer want to be. Of course in most cases the bigger the change the less time it will take you to achieve your goals.

Let me make this clear; there is an immense amount of information written and taught regarding the power of the mind and the connection between mind, body and soul. Literally, there are thousands of books, e-books, articles and scripts telling you how to get rich, how to be number one at work, how to perform at your peak in sports and in academia. All this shared knowledge is great but it is not quite so simple for everyone to learn how to utilize the power of the mind. After all, the mind is the most powerful instrument in the universe.

My intention for sharing this information that I have received through intense research, study and practice is to help you improve your life, and avoid a long and slow process to resolve personal issues or to achieve the goals you have set for yourself. All the information, knowledge, exercises, and tools that I share with you in this book is exactly the same information that I share and implement in my private practice every day.

Let's cut to the chase. Nobody knows more about you than yourself. Since all the experiences of your life are stored in your mind, you are the captain of your vessel. So, if you are trying to improve your life, first you want to learn and understand yourself in a deeper level before you can put your mind to work for you. It is very simple, a lot of people feel stuck, they keep doing the same thing over and over again and expecting different results. I will share with you the process to break out of this cycle.

When you begin processing information in a new way, you will be able to experience new things; you will start to open new doors and opportunities and you will be able to make the best of them. I will also show you how important is to take action; by putting into practice these actions steps you will increase your success and achievements. Remember no one else can take action for you, no matter how desperate your family and friends try to help, it is always up to you to take the initiative.

How it all began

My journey began with an interest in understanding the human mind. After years of searching different avenues and reading endless amount of literature, my search took me to the doors of the Institute of the Study of the Mind and Hypnotherapy in Miami, Florida. I decided to enroll on their hypnotherapy courses. The institute is very well known for it exceptional comprehensive curriculum, which includes philosophy, psychology, physiology, nutrition, esoteric teachings and more. The institute has been voted best hypnotherapy center several years in a row by the International Association

Introduction

of Counsellors and Therapists (IACT). I was very fortunate to have the opportunity to study under two great minds "Los Maestros" Professor Santiago Aranegui Ph.D. and Professor Flavio Campos Ph.D. I achieved my certification as a clinical hypnotherapist followed by certifications in Life Coaching and Master NLP (Neuro-Linguistic Programming) Practitioner from Bennett/Stellar University. TimeSlip therapy from the University of Wisconsin. Professionally trained in EMDR (Eye Movement Desensitization and Reprocessing) and IBSR (Integration Based Stress Reduction). Along the way I also achieved certifications as a Personal Trainer, Nutrition and Wellness Consultant, Weight Management Consultant, and Yoga fitness instructor (Presented here is a condensed description of my training).

As a Life Coach and practitioner of Hypnotherapy and Neuro-Linguistic Programming my career means so much more than just a source of income; I establish a partnership with every client. We are in the same team, engaged on a high stake chess game against one or several opponents. Who are these opponents? You may ask. The opponents are negative suggestions, programs, habits, or addictions. These opponents somehow along the line got implanted deep inside in the client's mind. My job is to take the pieces the client has on the board and help them make the right moves to get the desired outcome. It is very important to understand that everyone has issues, no matter how perfect the life of others might seem. Realize that the fact is very simple, everyone in this world is here to learn and evolve.

We are in a new millennium where we have to change, eventually everyone will understand and participate in this huge shift in collective consciousness. We need to leave behind the old way of life where we are constantly exhausted, always on the rush, trying to get things done. We need to take the time and look inwards and understand that we are living in a very special era, the old left brain analytical way of thinking won't be enough to handle this shift. You need to pay attention to your intuition, your dreams, your emotions to be able to stay positive, to protect yourself, and to attract all the right conditions to evolve as a human being and as a spiritual energy.

In recent times we have collectively conditioned ourselves to surf through hundreds of channels on TV, listen to music everywhere we go and spend countless hours downloading the latest videos or apps in our smart phones. We do all this to distract the mind from the body in order to relax or prevent boredom. Sadly, when we disconnect our minds from our bodies, we disassociate not only from what our body is doing but from how we feel mentally and emotionally.

It is time to make the conscious decision to switch our approach to life. The answer lies in the integration of mind and body; integration is the secret element for a gratifying, satisfactory and healthy lifestyle.

Always keep this book close to you, study it, refer to it. I hope with this knowledge you'll discover the path to success, happiness and the life you desire.

Part One
Watch Out For That First Step

Part One
The Power Of Listening

"Listening looks easy, but it's not simple. Every head is a world."
- Anonymous

Mastering Success

You probably think that you know yourself pretty well. You might be partially right on assuming this. After all only you know exactly what it is going on in your head. You are aware what motivates you and what makes you tick, or do you only think you know? Sometimes it can be very difficult for us to see and hear ourselves as we really are.

Now stop for a second and think hard; are you really listening to your inner voice, your internal monologue? Each of us has an inner voice that guides us as we move forward in our lives. One of the main focus in my private practice is to bring attention to this internal voice. The voice you are hearing may be your own but in some cases it might be a recorded voice of someone else playing repeatedly, telling you how to act or how to feel. In many cases it might be the voice of someone that is close to your heart.

As you attach feelings and thoughts to this voice, it is crucial that you pay attention to what your inner voice is telling you. If you find that some of these messages that are playing inside your head are negative or counter productive you need to find out the source. Listen to the tonality, pitch, loudness, distance and even direction (left or right side of your head).

Remember that most us listen to authoritative figures, our parents, teachers or even friends. Unfortunately a lot of the times they impose on us some of their limiting beliefs. Their voices are recorded in our subconscious mind, even from early age; these recordings will play over and over again under different circumstances, eventually creating patterns and overtime these patterns will develop into habits or behaviours.

I want you to realize that your subconscious mind is the largest data recorder in the universe and it has been recording every sight, sound, smell, taste, and feeling since you were born; never erasing any recorded memory. Now imagine this recording device playing a limiting belief that was planted somewhere along your life time. Unfortunately without listening and paying attention to these sounds, sights, or feelings, any situation or experience can trigger a negative memory in less than a millisecond, all of a sudden you are experiencing all sort of unpleasant emotions, setting in motion a self defeating program.

Fortunately your unconscious mind has also stored all of your accomplishments, your resources and strengths that are far more vast than you think. The same way that you taught yourself to trigger certain negative feeling and emotions under certain conditions, you can also train your mind to reverse the process and actually achieve a positive emotion and outcome under the same circumstances, it only requires for you to start listening.

As you acquire a greater insight into the way you think, you are tapping into the source of the causes, no longer paying attention to the manifestation and the effect. This is where you take control of your life, by listening. As you start taking control of your own life, you will adopt a higher standard for yourself; you'll set yourself free from any external influences. This way you will become empowered by being in charge of your own destiny.

Listening is the way one begins the process of self-awareness. It is very simple, all you need to do is give yourself the time, attention and commitment you deserve. This process will shift your point of view in life. You will function and deal with the causes that influence every decision and action you take. When you apply the *power of listening* in your life, you will rise above previous circumstances that have caused you stress, worries, frustration and even feelings of depression. You will see life in a new perspective; a life you deserve, where you no longer will be a pawn on a high stake chess game but a confident individual who has complete control of her/his life; this is self-empowerment.

To be empowered you need to make a commitment to succeed, to listen and take full responsibilities for your actions. You have to stop blaming others for your current state; don't blame yourself ether. Search within and discover what decisions and actions you took that brought you to the circumstances you find yourself at this point in your life.

Commit to make listening a top priority. This means believing you deserve a successful and healthy life. By making *the power of listening* a priority you become more open-minded and willing to pay attention to your own intuition. In other words this is the first step into developing your intuition.

By listening to your intuition you will find the purpose of your life and your place in the world. Once you listen to your inner voice you open the door to your unconscious mind, your Higher Self. By having access to your unconscious mind you are obtaining knowledge that is not available to the analytical conscious mind. The positive effect of this process will allow your life to flow with feelings of confidence and awareness which will manifest in your life as love, happiness, creativity, motivation, forgiveness and other positive emotions and experiences.

You might be already aware of the fact that the lessons we learn in our daily life become deeply rooted in our mind and are remembered longer and more vividly than the lessons we learn in school. It is essential for you to be aware of this fact, by having this in mind, you will now be aware that the lessons you learn from experiences go deeper than the lessons you learn in any seminar, workshop or classroom. This is why is so important to follow your "heart" and keep your eyes (the mind) open.

The Power Of Listening

Have you ever stopped and paid close attention to your own words when you are ready to make an important decision or any decision for that matter, do you tell yourself "I *have to* do this task," "I *must* find the answer," "I *should* finish my chores"? All these statements implies obligation, words and expressions such as "must, need, should, got to, have to, ought to" are associated with feelings of stress. So it is no surprise that whenever we begin a project where we use this type of expression, we either never finish it or we perform the task as a burden. From this point on, start switching all those obligation word for more empowering words, for example "I can, I want, I choose to, I desire, I love to." The way you express yourself will be the feelings you will experience.

Do you know the difference when you tell yourself or to others "I think, I can…" Versus "I feel, I can…"?. The difference is quite clear, "I think" is coming from the analytical conscious mind, "I feel" is coming from your unconscious mind, your Higher Self. Now you cannot have one without the other but it is very important that from now on you start paying close attention. By paying close attention you will start to make better decisions. For example you don't want to make a decision about love by focusing only on what you are thinking. You need to pay more attention to your feelings, to the heart. On the other hand you don't want to make a financial decision based only on your feelings. You need to think it over, the analytical conscious mind.

A lot of people have a distorted idea of what constitutes a good or bad decision because they don't listen to their inner-voice. By taking action without applying *the power of listening* it will be very hard improving the quality of your lifestyle. You must learn to hear yourself clearly, not through the voices of others but through your own voice. This is a task truly valuable, tap into this great resource and take control of your life.

The Power of Listening

Step 1.

If you are feeling bad, down or depressed, there are certain things you are doing internally. You will be either internally hearing negative suggestions, or seeing negative images, or physically feeling negative sensations or maybe even experiencing all three at the same time. Implement *the Power of Listening* and take notice of everything that is going on in your mind and body.

Step 2.

With your eyes closed or open, take a moment and mentally screen out any distractions. Listen to your thoughts and feelings to understand your emotional state. The important thing is to be attentive. If your thoughts start to wander, immediately concentrate and refocus.

Step 3.

Allow your mind to create a mental movie, a picture, or an arrangement of abstract symbols of the information being communicated that is making you feel bad.

Step 4.

Take this movie, picture or symbols and make it smaller, much smaller. To the size you can hardly see it, feel it or hear it. Imagine that it becomes so small that it turns into dust, powder, filth.

Step 5.

Now with your breath, blow from your mouth and visualize, imagine and feel that you blow the dust far away and the wind takes it all away, far away.

Step 6.

Next, call to mind a time in your life when you felt wonderful and inspired. Connect with all the feelings and emotions of that memory. See it clearly, hear it loudly, feel it intensely, just like you were there now. Once again implement *the Power of Listening* to strengthen those great feelings.

Step 7.

Visualize and imagine yourself experiencing all those great feelings tomorrow, next week and next month.

You Are What You Believe

"The sky is falling, The sky is falling."
- Chicken Licken

Mastering Success

As far as we know we are the only species on this planet that have the ability to believe. We can establish a believe just about anything. We believe in faith, justice, reason, politics, even in reality. Every person in the world is a belief generating machine. Unfortunately sometimes we take someone else's beliefs and adopt them as ours, some negative, some positive.

Did you know that your unconscious mind cannot recognize between negative and positive? It's true, just like the genie in the bottle, it only follows commands based on your programming (beliefs). It is very simple: if you shift your thinking, your life will shift; I can tell you without a single drop of a doubt that you can attract all the success you want in your personal life and in your professional life; keep in mind that every event, situation, fortune or misfortune that happens in your life is due to your own beliefs. It is not the outside world that is causing your failures or accomplishments; it is all the beliefs within you. You cannot blame anyone else, so you have to take responsibility for your own life.

When you get what you want or you don't get what you want, is your belief that generated that experience. For example: if you don't get that raise that you wanted or you get rejected by that person you wanted to date, it is your belief system that prevented you from achieving this goal. To make things worst, once a negative event like this happens you reenforce all those limiting beliefs by telling yourself phrases such as "This always happens to me," "This happened because I am too old," "I will never get this raise," "He/she is too good for me", "I am a failure." If you believe that you are a failure or that you don't deserve to achieve your goals, then you definitely will fail at attaining them.

Most people like to take credit for their accomplishment but prefer to blame someone else for their failures; don't delude yourself. You are making all this happen, whether in a positive or negative matter. For example: if you wish and believe that you are going to get promoted; when it does happen, you tell your friends and family "You see, I knew I was going to get it." It is very easy to give yourself credit. But, most people blame others when something negative happens; let's say you think and believe you cannot get promoted because your boss doesn't like you; when your boss announces that one of your coworkers got the promotion, you tell your family and friends "You see, I told you my boss didn't like me."

It is time for you to stop creating and feeding these limiting believes. Realize that consciously or unconsciously you are drawing everything that you don't want in your life. Take the first step and question yourself regarding these beliefs, for example: "Does this really happen to me all the time?" Probably not, I bet you can think of numerous times when you got what you wanted; "Do I really believe I will never get that raise?" I am pretty sure you know you can get that raise down the road, "Do I really believe that I am a failure?" You don't, just think of the many achievements in your life. Just like in a courtroom, answering the questions will show that these limiting beliefs are false, guilty of perjury.

Don't think for a moment that you are holding limiting beliefs all by yourself, everyone in the world has limiting beliefs. No matter how successful the life of someone else might seem, they too are wrestling with their own negative beliefs. If you want to get ahead in life, then your job is to identify and get rid of the most damaging and destructive beliefs. The only way to achieve this, is by replacing an old out of date belief with a new more useful and constructive belief. Our belief system is like the operating system in a computer. You cannot simply remove the operating system without replacing it with another updated version. Without an operating system the computer doesn't work. This new updated belief always has to be in the present tense, you have to believe that it's already a reality, it's a fact, something that you can see, hear and feel. If you believe that you will achieve a certain goal in six months or a year from today, then this belief has to be as true in your mind as you are sure that the sun will come up tomorrow morning. If you have any doubts or fears, you might not achieve it because you are taking all the energy away from it and placing it somewhere in an uncertain future.

Is always good to remember that wealth and happiness is not a thing, something concrete, or something you hold with your hand. Wealth and happiness is a belief. How do we know this? Is very simple; we know very well that if you take two individuals. One a successful millionaire, the other an honest individual that makes $25,000.00 a year. You take away all their possessions from them and place them in a foreign country without contacting anyone they know. If you look at their lives after a year, you will find that the millionaire is making more money than before and the individual that made $25,000.00 a year is working on a job that brings in about the same income as before. You might ask yourself, why? Very simple, deep inside the millionaire believes that he is worth over a million dollars, on the other hand the other individual believes he is worth $25,000.00. I recommend that you start believing that you are very valuable.

You can make some amazing achievements in you life as long as you are willing to believe you can. If you want to achieve better health, you have to believe that you are entitled to it. Learn how to use this powerful ability that you possess to enrich your life and the life of those near you. Never let anyone or anything break your belief system. Always have the persistence to keep believing. Whatever you do don't take any shortcuts and most important, don't fall in the trap of instant gratification. If you believe something is worth while, don't settle for something less. For instance, if you believe you can lose thirty pounds; don't be lured by claims and advertising that offers immediate results by taking a pill or by having an unnecessary surgery. Let me repeat myself, *don't take any shortcuts and don't fall in the trap of instant gratification*; if you do, most of the time you will regret it. For the example presented here, the proper way of achieving your goal of controlling your weight would be by eating healthy and exercising.

Believe in yourself as you move forward in life. Allow this knowledge to help you develop and advance your growth emotionally, mentally, physically, and spiritually. Open your mind and let your beliefs remove any obstacles in your path to success. You have all the resources you need to achieve what you want; the outcome of every action you take lies on the reality you choose to believe.

When you decide to make a shift in your belief system always make sure you see it and feel it, starting from the present moment and in action for the rest of your life. Follow the steps on the following exercise, to implement the changes you want to achieve in your life.

Shift Your Believes

Step 1.

Select a spot where you will not be disturbed for about ten minutes. With your palms facing upward place your hands loosely on your lap. Take three deep breaths and allow yourself to relax.

Step 2.

Determine a limiting belief that you want to get rid of. Elicit all the negative feelings, sensations and emotions from that belief. Picture any moment in your past where this limiting belief prevented you from achieving your goal.

Step 3.

Imagine you can hold this picture in one of your hands. Notice all the details in the picture. See it, hear it, feel it.

Step 4.

Now, think of a useful belief you want to have in your life. Elicit all the positive feelings, sensations and emotions from this belief. Imagine a time in the future where this new positive belief allowed you to achieve your goal.

Step 5.

Imagine you can hold this picture of yourself in the future in the opposite hand. Notice all the details in the picture. See it, hear it, feel it.

Step 6.

Look back at your hand where you are holding the picture with the limiting belief. As you look at it, the picture is becoming dull looking, notice how the picture becomes blurry and white out, slowly shrinking down, smaller and smaller to the point that you can no longer see it, hear it or feel it.

Step 7.

Go back to the opposite hand where you are holding the new useful and positive belief you want in your life. Look closely; allow the picture to become larger and larger, with brighter and sharper tones. Imagine the picture becoming so large that it takes up all the space in front of you. You actually need both hands to hold it. See it, hear it, feel it and believe it. Repeat this exercise three to four times and increase the effect.

Take Action

"We live in a universe of action."
- Santiago Aranegui

Mastering Success

I am going to make a bold statement "The most important element in our life is *action*". Planning, imagining, and visualization are essential but *action* is without a doubt the most important element of the equation. It is true that the universe is constantly supporting every single thought and request we send to it but nothing would materialize without the crucial step of taking action "set the wheels in motion".

Imagination is the cause of creation, next you visualize with more details what you desire, and last you take action to materialize what you planned. Do you realize that the opposite of depression and boredom is action. Most people take their actions, or lack of it, for granted. Your own well being and your abilities to accomplish things depend upon taking action, no matter how simple or complex your goal is.

All successful individuals in any profession have one thing in common, they take action. In fact the ability to take action is perhaps the single most important skill you could ever acquire. Taking action is a greater factor than intelligence, connections, luck (if you believe in such a thing as luck) or talent.

You know very well that one of the laws of the universe is that we don't get something for nothing. Everyone must take action to earn the physical, emotional, mental and spiritual development we seek. There are no big secrets, no shortcuts. There are a lot of people that are tricked and mislead by false ideas or hidden agendas that promise immediate personal development or instant solutions to their problems. Don't allow yourself to fall into this trap.

One of the main issues most of my clients struggle with is this crucial step. They do well in imagining and visualizing themselves performing and achieving the desired personal goals but for some reason or another they don't take action.

Take Action

You probably have heard the old saying "Actions speak louder than words." I'm pretty sure you also heard a number of people saying "I am going to do it" or "I will start tomorrow" but they never do. These people are always waiting to start until things are perfect, which probably never will be; for some of these individuals things are never quite right. The economy is bad, the market is down, or the competition is too tough. By now you know very well there is no perfect time to start, you have to take action now.

Don't get me wrong, planning is important, but a well organized plan is only valuable after you take action to implement it. Winston Churchill wrote "I never worry about action, but only inaction" that is precisely the point. An average idea that's been put into action is worth more than a thousand profound ideas that are on hold for "The perfect time" or "For the right opportunity."

If you have a plan that you really believe in, it is time for you to do something about it; concentrate on what you can do in the present moment. Don't worry about what happened last week or what might be ahead tomorrow. The only time you can take action is in the present. There is nothing more devastating to your dreams and goals than the idea that yesterday determines the present and that the future is a mysterious place full of dangerous unknowns.

Contrary to popular belief, action is the best cure for fear. Do you remember the first time you rode a bicycle or your first day at school? It is a fact that the most difficult time to take action is the very first time you embark in a new project, but after you find the courage and set the wheels on motion, you become confident and things always get better and easier. So take action on all those brilliant ideas you have and get rid of any doubts and fears you have experienced in the past.

Mastering Success

The best way to develop a pattern of taking action is to rely on yourself instead of others. You need to set your own standards and principles and move forward accordingly; you need to be completely honest with yourself. Set up a plan with a specific date to take action and begin your project. A lot of people have the tendency to procrastinate, to leave things for "later" but unfortunately many times "later" never comes, so find ways to stay motivated and take action.

Once you create this habit of taking action you will become more consistent in achieving all your goals (short term and long term goals). Over time you will develop accountability not for others but for yourself, you will take action without making an effort. It will become second nature to you. People will start to wonder why you can achieve your goals so easily. Some might even say that you are a very "lucky" person, but you know luck has nothing to do with your accomplishments. The reason behind this is very simple: Your motivation and drive comes from within, outside circumstances and events have little to no effect on your success.

Taking action will have an incredible impact in your personal and professional life, you will feel good about yourself. Like many things in life, becoming skillful at taking action is all in your mind. Sometimes you might forget that it is in your nature to be active, that energy flows through your whole body, mind and soul. It is like a river of life flowing through you and the only way to release this energy is by taking action.

I always remember an old Aesop fable that I read when I was a kid. Did you ever read or watch the cartoon version of The Ant and the Grasshopper? Well the fable goes something like this:

Once there lived an ant and a grasshopper in a grassy meadow. The ant worked hard in the summer's heat, collecting grains from

Take Action

the farmer's field. All day long he would work, without resting, scurrying back and forth, collecting the grains and storing them carefully in his home.

The grasshopper thought that the ant was a fool. He laughs, dances and plays the whole summer away, often asking "Why do you work so hard?" "Come and rest for awhile, listen to my song and lets dance all day." The ant ignored him and kept working.

The summer turned into fall, and fall into winter. It became freezing cold, and it began to snow. At that moment the grasshopper remembered the ant. He had no food or shelter, so he dies out in the cold.

Of course the moral of the story is: Be responsible and take action. Never leave that till tomorrow which you can do today. So, I advise you to think like the ant. Ignore all the negative and discouraging grasshoppers around you.

Let me share with you a great insight that my professor Flavio S. Campos taught me and I get to see it almost every day in my private practice: *"You want to live in the present. People that are depressed tend to focus on the past. People with generalized anxiety disorder are constantly focusing on the future and in both cases it has a negative effect in the present."* You can clearly appreciate the wisdom of his words. His message is simple, do not allow any regrets from the past or fear of the future hold you back from taking action today. Don't sit back and let your life pass you by; you have the potential to make your live better, *take action*, you won't regret it.

Follow the steps on the following exercise, to be more confident and motivated to take action.

Take Action

Step 1.

Select a spot where you will not be disturbed for about ten minutes. Take three deep breaths and allow yourself to relax. Think about the most important goal you want to achieve. Imagine how you'd like to be really motivated to take action. The goal you pursue needs to be highly desirable. In other words it has to be important to you, it needs to spark a fire within you.

Step 2.

Now, think back to a time in the past when you were really motivated. Think about how you took action on that motivation and achieved the desired goal. Recall that event and make the pictures bigger, brighter and more colourful. Feel what you felt at that moment. Imagine that you can absorb the energy of that motivation and action into your body.

Step 3.

Make the emotions and sensations stronger and stronger, keep increasing the feeling. Run this mental story over and over again, each time more vividly.

Step 4.

As the feelings increase, rub the thumb of your dominant hand in the palm of your other hand. As you do so, imagine stepping into your own body and experience that moment as if you were reliving that experience once again. Connect with all those great feelings.

Step 5.

Now, while you're still rubbing your palm, switch back and think about your most important goal you want to achieve in the future. Imagine accomplishing that goal exactly the way that you want to.

Step 6.

Keep rubbing your palm, visualize from this point on that anytime you want to be highly motivated and ready to take action, all you have to do, is just rub your palm.

Step 7.

Check the final outcome. Does the goal fit with other goals you have? Does the goal meet your standard? Will achieving this goal enhance your life? Does it empower you? If you are satisfied with the results, you can release this visualization. If you find any negative factors, you need to start from step one and modify the end result. Repeat this exercise three to four times or until you can experience the feeling of motivation every time you rub your palm.

Part Two
You Have All The Answers

Understanding

"Only the development of compassion and understanding for others can bring us the tranquillity and happiness we all seek."
- Dalai Lama XIV

In order to understand others you must understand yourself. The first step in understanding yourself is to learn the way you process information. As human beings we are fortunate to have the ability to examine ourselves. Unfortunately this process is avoided by a lot of people. This is a gift we all have and some of us take it for granted, the same way we take for granted breathing fresh air or eating healthy. If you read the second chapter "You are what you believe," you should have a clear understanding that there is a continuous flow of information that is being filtered by our beliefs. By now you should also know that our beliefs make us who we are.

So, how do you start understanding yourself and others? It is very simple. Let me ask you something, how do you find out what someone else wants? You ask. Questions hold the power to make us think and the answers to those questions give us the ability to understand. Since we know that nobody knows more about yourself that you. Then is time for you to start asking yourself some important questions.

The following questions cover the seven essential areas in life: Career, Environment, Finances, Fun, Health, Relationships, Spirituality. Don't be afraid to go in depth as you answer these questions. They are quite simple, so simple that you may ask, "How is answering these questions going to help me understand myself?" Do not ignore them; once you start searching for the answers you will tap into your subconscious mind. This will bring you the understanding you are seeking.

Find a comfortable spot where you won't be disturbed. Take a piece of paper and a pen to write down the questions and your answers. Remember there is no right or wrong answer, write down whatever comes to mind and do yourself a favor. Don't answer the questions with a simple yes or no; don't censor your feelings and emotions, so let's get started.

Understanding

- *Career:*

"What do you think is your true calling?"
"If you could have your dream job what would it be?"
"What do you need to do to realize your dream job?"
"How would achieving your dream job affect you and the people around you?"
"Where do you see yourself in one year?"
"Do you believe in yourself?"
"What is stopping you?"

- *Environment:*

"How do the things you own enhance your life?"
"How do the things you own hurt your life?"
"What in your environment exhausts your energy?"
"What is the one "thing" you could not live without?"
"If you could make a change in your living environment, what would it be?"
"What does your living environment says about you?"
"What is stopping you from achieving your ideal living environment?"

- *Finances:*

"What are your money values?"
"How are your finances right now?"
"How can you improve financially?"
"How do you see yourself one year from today financially?"
"Is there anything draining you financially?"
"How long before you can achieve your financial goal?"
"What is stopping you from achieving your financial goal?"

- *Fun:*

"What makes you smile?"
"What activities did you enjoy doing in the past?"
"What are your favorite things to do in the present?"
"What activities make you feel like you are wasting your time?"

"What activities are you good at?"
"What is the one fun thing you always wanted to do but haven't done?"
"What is stopping you from doing the activities you want to do?"

• *Health:*
"How is your health?"
"How many hours do you sleep?"
"Do you consider yourself to be under stress?"
"How active you are on a daily basis?"
"Do you get enough exercise?"
"What do you need to do to take better care of yourself?"
"What is stopping you from achieving a healthy lifestyle?"

• *Relationships:*
"Are you satisfied with your family/romantic relationship?"
"How is you relationship with your family"
"Do you feel that you need some space or time alone?"
"Do you feel that your emotional needs are not being met? If not, why not?"
"What is the best thing about your family/romantic life?"
"What are your commitments to your family/romantic relationship?"
"What is stopping you from achieving a healthy family/romantic relationship?"

• *Spirituality:*
"When do you feel highly spiritual?"
"What does spirituality mean to you?"
"What is your ideal state of spirituality?"
"What is missing in your spiritual life?"
"How can you achieve the level of spirituality you desire?"
"What is stopping you from achieving the level of spirituality you desire"

Understanding

Now take a moment to review your answers. Keep in mind that these questions are meant to explore and understand your current situation. Asking gets more information out in the open and forces you to realize what is going on internally. In most cases, just the act of seeking for an answer and thinking things through in a organized way will bring to light the solution to any issue you want to resolve or any goals you want to achieve.

Understanding yourself is the objective you want to accomplish. Once you have achieved this, understanding others is much easier. Start asking yourself the right questions so you can have a clear and specific goal from where to start.

Find Yourself

Step 1.

Find a place where you will not be disturbed for about 30 minutes. Sit in a straight back chair. Close your eyes and take three deep easy breaths to relax yourself. Continue to relax, breathing easily and naturally.

Step 2.

Imagine you are moving forward in a long peaceful and safe dark tunnel. The tunnel can look like anything you want. It can have flowers on the ground, beautiful gems on the wall and ceiling. Notice that in the distance there is a door at the end of this tunnel.

Step 3.

Imagine that this door will take you into the future, your seventy-fifth birthday to be more exact. Count to seven, and imagine yourself standing in front of the door. Notice all the details of the door in front of you, the more details the better. Put your hand on the door knob. Open the door, step through the door.

Step 4.

Visualize all your family members and friends have organised this party for you, to show you how much they love you. Take a few minutes to pay close attention to all the details, sounds, and sensations. Concentrate on this new environment.

Step 5.

Imagine that each person at your party is telling something about your life. Stories about your accomplishments, describing the kind of person you are. Pay close attention to what everyone is saying. What would you like them to say about you?

Step 6.

Once you are satisfied and heard what you needed to hear, imagine thanking everyone for being present at such a wonderful occasion. Slowly start walking back to the door and back through the tunnel. Count to three and open your eyes. You will feel wide awake, refreshed, and very positive about what you have just experienced.

Step 7.

Spend more time with those who love and support your growth in all of the seven essential areas in life: Career, Environment, Finances, Fun, Health, Relationships, Spirituality.

Acceptance

"Happiness can exist only in acceptance."
- George Orwell

There are many definitions for the word *acceptance*. For example it can mean the act of receiving something offered (Gift, offering, etc.) It can also mean the agreement of a contract. But the definition or concept of the word acceptance that I am referring to is much more profound, for you see acceptance also implies a *non-judgmental mindset*.

Unfortunately every one in this planet has been "taught" (programmed to be more exact) to judge others. We judge people by their appearance, social status, religion, ethnicity, actions, and just about everything else we can think of. In fact some "experts" hypothesise that we are actually hard-wired to be judgmental.

We live in a society that thrives on judging and criticizing others. You can turn the TV on and find countless programs that are nothing more than engines of criticism. They chastise and slander everyone, from the way they dress to the way they eat, nothing is left out. These self proclaimed fashion or news experts don't even care about age or gender, because everyone is going to be harshly judged.

I understand that everyone is entitled to have "their own opinion" but what I want you to comprehend is that any judgmental thoughts you have are actually affecting you in a negative way physically, mentally and spiritually. Have you noticed how much time we actually spend judging and criticising other people? Even love ones. The truth is, that most conversations that we engage are about judging other people. Take a moment and just think how often we sit down around the table at home and talk about someone at work or at school; how about on the phone? I am pretty sure just about everyone has picked up the phone to call or text their best friend to tell them how awful certain person looked or behaved.

Acceptance

We all know how much judgement and criticism can hurt us. What you might not realize is that judging others actually is very damaging to our confidence and self esteem. Taking pleasure at the expense of others feeds into your ego and the truth is that your ego is totally dependent on external approval. So you see, the more you feed your ego the more you will depend on it and the more you depend on it the more you will have to endure it. This is what I call the *Ego Trap*. I will touch very briefly on the Ego Trap, since this is a very large subject that could no doubt be a book itself.

Have you ever felt your ego? You might not realize it but you actually have. You know that feeling of emptiness that you feel inside you from time to time. Well, that is your ego. This emptiness is manifested in many different ways, for example: some people feel that they don't belong in this world. Others feel that they cannot connect with other people. Some feel a big empty hole inside and others feel a deep and dull pain or discomfort within. Sadly people will do anything to fill the emptiness.

Some people even develop additions to alcohol, drugs, food, sex, shopping, work, and just about anything else to temporarily fill the black hole inside. Let me explain, our ego always wants more, so people seek instant gratification, that is the trap. Our ego deceives us by finding short term solutions, knowing very well that sooner or later we will need to come back and rely on it again, only to repeat the cycle. Sometimes the feeling of emptiness is so overwhelming that people experience a feeling of entrapment or a sensation of having no way out, to the point of having suicidal tendencies.

This is where *acceptance* comes in. When we accept the world as it is and we accept ourselves just the way we are, we open the doors to a more joyful life. If you embrace a lifestyle of acceptance you begin to connect with people in a deeper level because you see them for who they really are, no matter the color of their skin, ethnicity, nationality, social status, etc. It's at this point that you see that no one is inherently better than anyone else; we are all just a bit different, unique, and special.

As you incorporate acceptance into your lifestyle, you end up enjoying every moment and encounter since everyone you meet has so much to offer. You'll free yourself from the restraints of judging people as good or bad, poor or rich, too old or too young, etc. Instead, you move forward on a new path towards seeing the best qualities in everyone.

I want you to keep in mind and put into practice the concept of acceptance. Next time you meet a friend at the mall or at a restaurant, I want you to defer from judging or criticizing people. If for some reason you need to make a statement about someone based on their character, make sure you always keep it positive. There is a difference between feedback and criticism; feedback is always beneficial for both the giver and the receiver. On the other hand criticism is always negative and judgmental, it is harmful for both.

If you follow the path of acceptance you will reap the rewards of a healthy lifestyle for the rest of your life; over time it will become second nature. You no longer will be concerned with what other people wear or how much they have. In fact all those things that used to annoy you so much are going to seem so trivial that you will wonder why they ever mattered.

Have you ever owned a dog? There is a reason why dogs are considered man's and woman's best friend (Contrary to advertising, diamonds are not a woman's best friend). Dogs are the epitome of absolute acceptance. It doesn't matter if we are black or white, rich or poor, mean or kind, they accept you unconditionally. Have you ever walked around in a large city

Acceptance

and seen a homeless person and next to him or her occasionally you might see a loyal dog laying down or sitting close to their owner. They don't run down the street after the guy in the hundred thousand dollar car, they accept their owner for who they are, no matter what.

Now, I'm not advocating for people to be like dogs. I'm simply making the point that accepting people (including yourself) will allow you to experience a greater personal growth. When you accept others, your focus changes from them to you, which will allow you to concentrate on improving yourself.

Always keep in mind that you cannot control the behaviour or actions of other people, so accepting people as they are does not mean you have to like them or overlook their unpleasant ways. Simply accept that it is the way they are and that you can't change them, so don't waste your time and energy.

Follow the steps on the following exercise, to start a lifestyle of acceptance.

Find Yourself

Step 1.

Find a place where you will not be disturbed for about 30 minutes. Sit in a straight back chair. Close your eyes and take seven deep easy breaths to relax yourself. Continue to relax, breathing easily and naturally.

Step 2.

Think how much you would like to achieve a lifestyle of acceptance or releasing any old habit like judging or criticising other people.

Step 3.

Now, visualize a person, living or deceased, whom you think would make a great mentor. Someone special that could assist you in creating a strong belief system that you can achieve this goal.

Step 4.

Imagine that you can speak to your mentor, and explain in detail what you want to achieve. If you have any doubts in achieving this goal, express it to him or her.

Step 5.

Imagine that your mentor very kindly and graciously encourages you to explore different and positive avenues to achieve your desired goal. Focus on all the options you and your mentor can come up with.

Step 6.

Once you have decided on the best path to take, visualize that your mentor is guiding you every step of the way, until you have reached your goal, just the way you want to.

Step 7.

Notice the improvement during the next few days. If by any reason something is unsatisfactory. Repeat the exercise again until you achieve a satisfactory result.

Forgiveness

"Forgiveness is the key to action and freedom."
- Hannah Arendt

I often ask people, what do you want in life? From time to time I get an answer like "I want a large house" or "I want to have a lot of money in the bank." It is very easy to understand why some people would respond this way, after all there is nothing wrong with wanting to acquire nice things in life. I for one encourage people to aspire to obtain what their hearts desire. In fact, it is your given right as a citizen in this world to be successful and enjoy everything that life has to offer. However, sooner or later people that keep pushing for or even achieving these goals, such as acquiring a mansion or having a large amount of money in the bank realize that they want more and more. They get caught up in an endless self-defeating and pointless pursuit.

But there are other people that answer this same question very wisely. Their answer is so simple, that sometimes is very hard to grasp the profound message behind it. So, what is this wise answer you may ask? Are you ready? (Drum roll) "I want to find peace" there you have it; I know you might be disappointed with the answer but just stop for a moment and analyse what this phrase actually implies "I want to find peace."

Peace is the state you achieve when you stop trying to acquire something or to trying get to some place. Inner peace allows you to live in the present. You are able to enjoy every aspect of life, both personally and professionally. Living peacefully in the present moment provides deep meaning to everything; you are able to let go of the past since you cannot ever change it and you dissolve any worries about the future.

Allow me to share an analogy that my good friend Dr. Gonzalez MD gave after one of his lectures. This is exactly how it happened; very casually he walked up to this man and looked at him straight into his eyes and told him the following:

"What happened in the past is already gone and you need to

move forward, it's just like driving. Imagine yourself driving a car on the highway. You are concentrating on the road ahead, if you don't you will crash, from time to time you will glance at the rear view mirror and look at what is behind you. That is life, you stay in the present but you're always moving forward and from time to time you glance back at your past."

A very wise and simple analogy that depicts the essence of living in the present. You might be asking yourself what does inner peace and living in the present have to do with forgiveness? You see, forgiveness is the key to inner peace and living in the present. It is forgiveness that heals all wounds not time. Forgiveness lets you enjoy an emotional, mental and physical healthy life. Forgiveness empowers you.

Have you ever heard, read or taken the course in miracles. The course in miracles at its core is a metaphysical study that teaches the path to ultimate love and peace through forgiving. You might not realize but when you forgive someone that has hurt you at any point in your life, you are the one who receives the most benefit from forgiveness, not the other person. In reality we have no choice but to forgive. What are the options after all, holding a grudge? When you hold a grudge your whole mind and body fills with anger, bitterness and hate. All those negative emotions and thoughts that you experience stir everything inside of you, eventually draining all the joy out of your life.

Lets face it, it's impossible to have peace when all that is on your mind is the thought that someone has hurt you or taken advantage of you; don't allow the heavy burden that a grudge creates, because it will hold you down. Grudges not only affect us negatively mentally and emotionally but just like all things that stress us out, in time it will cause illness in our bodies.

I share with all my clients the knowledge and practical techniques I have acquired to resolve serious issues to allow the process of forgiveness and healing to begin. Some of my clients have held on to grudges and negative emotions for decades. In some cases they are bitterly angry at people that had passed away many years ago. Sometimes forgiving takes time, and in some cases it can happen overnight; when the latter happens it is very common for the person to experience an incredible feeling of relief, like a huge weight or pressure has been taken off.

Forgiveness is the only way to free ourselves. The following is a case study where forgiveness allowed the client to free herself from years of sadness and anger. The name of the client has been changed to protect her privacy.

Jessica described herself as a successful career woman. She always arrived on time and waited patiently if I was still in a session. Consistently she suffered from headaches. She explained that she had suffered this way since she was a child. Nothing the doctors had prescribed seemed to help ease the pain.

There had been several sessions over the span of four weeks. Jessica had disclosed that her older sister called her almost every day to check up on her and to let her know what she should be doing. Jessica's sister would "advise" her constantly on anything from the way she should dress to whom she should date.

Jessica loved her sister and had a good relationship with her. So during this particular session, which ended up being a crucial session*, I asked Jessica to sit back and relax. After achieving a deep state of relaxation (hypnotic state), she was able to uncover a deep feeling of resentment and bitterness towards her sister. Deep inside she begrudged her sister because she felt she always manipulated her life.

Through various therapeutic modalities Jessica was able to forgive

Forgiveness

her sister. The session was concluded and she emerged from hypnosis. During the following weeks Jessica reported that for some unknown reason her sister no longer called her every day. In fact she only called during the weekends and the dynamics of the conversations had also changed. Very gladly she also mentioned that her headaches had vanished.

Jessica changed her relationship with her sister when she was able to forgive her. What it is interesting is the fact that her sister was not present during the therapy. Forgiveness not only leads you to healing and inner-peace but it also leads the other person or individuals that you forgave on the same path.

If you are willing to forgive, consider the following steps below:

---

* *In coaching and hypnotherapy there is always a crucial session where there is a major breakthrough.*

Forgiving

Step 1.

Make a mental list of those people who have hurt or offended you, whether they are alive or have passed away.

Step 2.

Find a place where you will not be disturbed for about 30 minutes. Sit in a straight back chair. Close your eyes and take seven deep easy breaths to relax yourself. Continue to relax, breathing easily and naturally. Repeat the word "relax" again and again, slowly allowing yourself to feeling more relaxed with each occurrence.

Step 3.

You are now going to create your own peaceful place. This place can be a real place where you have been before or a place you just created. In this peaceful place you are completely safe and secure. You are totally in control, relaxed and empowered. Nobody can enter this place unless you choose to allow them in. Connect with this place.

Step 4.

Take the time to be in this place with no worries, bitterness, anger or concerns. You know that everything is just the way that it needs to be. Connect with the peace within, with your Higher Self; visualize your Higher Self as a bright light in front of you.

Step 5.

Ask your Higher Self to release all anger, bitterness, grudges or sadness. Take a deep breath, as you exhale, imagine releasing away from you a dark fog or smoke, symbolizing all those negative energy and emotions. Repeat mentally the word "Clear" three times. Keep releasing this dark negative energy away from your body and mind until you can only see, feel and hear clean, clear and refreshing air as you exhale.

Step 6.

Once you sense you have released all those negative emotions, visualize as you breathe in, a healing white light entering your mind, body and soul bringing enjoyment, love, forgiveness and happiness. Feel, see and hear the light filling your entire being; see yourself completely surrounded by the light. Now visualize clearly the person or people that hurt or offended you in the pass. By the act of forgiveness share the healing white light with this person or these people.

Step 7.

When you are done sharing the healing light, look at them in the face and tell them that you forgive them. Once you are done, thank your Higher Self for giving you the strength to forgive others. Count to seven and open your eyes. You will feel wide awake, refreshed, and very positive about what you have just experienced.

Part Three
Who Is That In The Mirror?

Our Thoughts

"Whether you think you can or whether you think you can't, you are right."
- Henry Ford

Thoughts are the most powerful mechanism in the universe. The content of thoughts change from context to context. It doesn't matter if it is in your personal life or your professional life. When you have a thought, your mind immediately starts searching for a solution to achieve the specific goal in relationship to the way you direct it and it doesn't matter if it is a positive or a negative thought. Your mind in one way or another will find the solution. For example: if the thought of getting fired from your job "pops" into your head, your mind will go in search of all the things that could go wrong. You probably will start visualizing or telling yourself negative suggestions such as "I will go broke," "It's going be difficult to find another job," "I will make less money," "I am too young or too old." All these adverse suggestions will trigger a wide range of negative emotions and feelings such as anxiety, stress and fear. If these thoughts go unchecked and you don't do anything to stop them they could develop into very serious problems such as phobias or depression. Eventually the original thought of getting fired will manifest itself, a self-fulfilling prophecy.

Always keep in mind how powerful your thoughts are; remember, you are what you think. So you have to switch your thought process from negative to positive. Take the same example presented above: instead of thinking what would happen if you get fired, you need to concentrate and think how much value you bring to company you work for. See yourself growing or continuing to work in this company. Your mind will go searching for all the things to keep you employed. You will start to visualize or telling yourself suggestions such as "I can make the company grow by doing..." "I will bring more value to my position by..." "I will improve productivity by..." With these positive suggestions you will be creating powerful feelings of confidence and self-assurance. Confidence is one of the most important personal qualities for success because it plays a major role in how people view you as an individual and in

Our Thoughts

what they believe about your performance. So by making this crucial thought pattern switch you materialize opportunities where others only saw a dead end.

Let me point out to you that the more intense your emotions, feelings and desires are, the more accurate and successful your goal will manifest, in a positive or negative way, you decide. For this reason the first consideration for you should be the acquirement of the appropriate attitude. Do your best to always develop the spirit of success and prosperity; emotionally you should feel empowered, this is another way to tell your subconscious mind exactly what you want.

Thoughts not only affect the outcome of conditions in the world around you but it has even a more profound effect on your body; your thoughts can have a profound effect on your health. The way you think has a direct connection of what goes on in your body. For every thought you have there is a biochemical response that is released in your body, this is a result of your thought. Let me give you a couple of examples, one positive and one negative:

Positive thoughts: You are home by yourself, and you recall a particular thought of joy. Your subconscious mind automatically sends a message to your body to release a particular chemical; in this instance would be serotonin "the happy hormone." You continue part of your day feeling cheerful.

Negative thoughts: You are sleeping and all of the sudden you hear a loud noise in the kitchen. Your mind goes into the flight or fight mode. Your subconscious mind immediately tells your brain to release several hormones. Two of these hormones that are released in your body are norepinephrine and adrenaline. All of the sudden your heartbeat and respiration speeds up, your muscles tense up, your pupils dilate, you experience tunnel vision, you might even start shaking. All this happens in a fraction of a second. You finally release all these stress, once you find out that there is no threat. You are relieved, it was just the cat making a mess in the kitchen.

As you can appreciate, your thoughts are creating the physical equivalent of what is going on in your mind. So every thought you have is affecting your body at the cellular level. If you don't want to take my word for it, ask your doctor or do some research on the *placebo effect; the latest research finds shows that the placebo effect account for 33% of the success in a treatment. Now you might realize that you really have to be in tune with the thoughts you are having. When it comes down to your health, you need to create positive thoughts of what you consider to be your ideal health.

So the right attitude is necessary. Start thinking of yourself as a healthy and strong person, and connect those thoughts with feelings. When you connect feelings with your thoughts, your mind automatically sends the message to your brain. Then your brain sends the message to the corresponding organ or gland to release those chemicals throughout your body. Research has shown that optimism has a powerful and positive effect on people's lives. If you are experiencing a particular discomfort or pain, you want to think that you are energetic, that you are flexible and recall memories when you were experiencing good health. Don't engage in thoughts of what you don't want, for example, "I don't want to feel pain", "I don't want to be ill any more." You always redirect your thought to what you want, "I want to feel comfortable," "I want to be healthy".

It helps to interact in activities that make you feel good, with a sense of purpose. This doesn't mean that you need to be involved in humanitarian or volunteering work, if you do, that is great. But just being involved in your favorite hobby will lift

Our Thoughts

your spirit up. Take the time to think, find what makes you happy in life.

* Placebo Effect: The beneficial effect in a patient following a particular treatment that arises from the patient's expectations concerning the treatment rather than from the treatment itself.

The American Heritage® Dictionary of the English Language, Fourth Edition copyright ©2000 by Houghton Mifflin Company. Updated in 2009. Published by Houghton Mifflin Company. All rights reserved.

Release Unwanted Thoughts

Step 1.

Find a place where you will not be disturbed for about 10 minutes. Sit in a straight back chair. Close your eyes and take three deep easy breaths to relax yourself. Continue to relax, breathing easily and naturally.

Step 2.

Notice any negative thoughts or feeling that are running through your mind. Find the emotions that are associated with these thoughts and feelings (sad, anger, etc).

Step 3.

Visualize an open box right in front of you, observe all the details about the box, the size, the color, the texture, etc. Imagine that you place all those negative thoughts, feelings and emotions inside the box; place a heavy lid on top of it and lock it.

Step 4.

Imagine setting the box on fire, see, feel and hear the fire; imagine the flames as orange color. Notice how the fire melts and evaporates the box and everything inside it.

Step 5.

Repeat the following word "Clear" seven times.

Step 6.

Next, imagine the wind taking the ashes far away, very far away. Notice the different feelings you are experiencing; increase the feeling over and over again.

Step 7.

Now think of a time in the future where you are applying these good feelings. See and feel yourself taking steps that will actually direct you toward your goal. In the following days after this exercise, notice what resources and answers your subconscious mind brings forward. Repeat this exercise every time you are feeling down or stuck.

Our Words

"All our words are but crumbs that fall down from the feast of the mind."
- Kahlil Gibran

Have you ever heard the old saying? "Sticks and stones may break my bones. But words may never hurt me". It is true that I wouldn't like a stick or a stone hitting me anywhere in my body but in a many cases words can be more hurtful than any physical injury. Painful words can have a lasting negative effect both physical and psychologically, especially coming from someone you love or trust. These negative effects can last for a very long time. Sometimes the person can never overcome the impression that those hurtful words made on him or her, therefore they suffer constantly for a whole lifetime.

The fact is "Our words can move mountains." Your words have the power of lifting a person out of the deepest depression and change her/his whole view on life, or they can have the worst devastating impact possible. You multiply the effect of your words by a hundred when you are addressing a child. In my practice I often hear people proudly say that they've never hit their child in an effort to justify how they speak to them, for example "I never laid a hand on my child but I let her know she is a disappointment to the whole family." These words can be so devastating to anybody but for a child, it can leave a deep psychological scar.

Do you know there are two main methods of programming the mind? One is by shock (Trauma, fear, injury, etc.) The other is through repetition. If you tell anybody the same phrase over and over during a period of time they will eventually believe it. For example, if you tell your child the following phrase "You can't do anything right," you are actually implanting this suggestion in your child's subconscious mind; this suggestion in time becomes a belief. This limiting belief about themselves becomes ingrained in their minds and will continue to run automatically as a subconscious program throughout their life.

We all know that most of the time people says these things not

Our Words

to hurt their loved ones but to actually encourage a change of behaviour. Unfortunately criticism is the worst way to address any issue. So from now on, you must learn to be more aware of the words that you use to address people, most importantly addressing young people.

Allow me to share a list of phrases to look for, when you are in the process of changing the way you approach people, especially children.

• *Comparing:*
"Why can't you be more like _____."
"If you could only be more like _____."
"Look how well _____ can get along with others."

Comparing does not help change behaviour. It can create a lot of pressure. For a child it can be very confusing and can damage their self-esteem. Comparing anyone to someone else implies that you wish they were different.

• *Rejection:*
"Don't bother me, I'm busy right now."
"I have to finish this one thing, we can talk later."
"See what you did, leave me alone, I don't want to see you."

Phrases like these can send a message of rejection. The feeling of rejection is terrible, no matter who is rejecting whom but when it comes from a parent, it is ten times more painful. If there is a behaviour that needs correcting, use appropriate discipline techniques but make sure to discuss the child's behaviour and the reason for the discipline.

• *Labelling:*
"You are just like_____"
"She is my lazy one."

"He is the troublemaker of the family"

Always remember that everyone is unique. Your children have different skills and personalities so it can seem natural to give them labels, but placing labels can limit your child's potential. A negative label can cut deeply; many adults can still recall vividly and bitterly when their own parents made a shameful statement about them.

• *Threatening:*
"I will give you something to cry about"
"Wait until we get home"
"You better do it or else"

Threats don't work. It's true that you can temporarily achieve certain behavioural changes with threats, but eventually your child will confront you. Let's face it, the fact is that sooner or later you will have to make good on those threats or else they loose their power, and where does that path leads to?

• *Judging:*
"You are a bad person"
"She is just awful"
"He is the worst person I know"

We've been taught from a young age to judge (criticize) other people, even our loved ones. We judge everyone on many different things, for example: character, appearance, values, status, etc. Of course there is also positive judgement but when we judge in a negative way it can be very upsetting, destructive, and painful.

These are just a few of the type of expressions that you need to watch out for. Once you become conscious of the way you express yourself you will immediately notice a change in how other people respond to you. Also remember that communication is not only verbal but also includes body language (Facial expressions, body posture, etc.) Therefore the path to effective communication begins with mindfulness.

In my line of work as a Life Coach, ninety percent of all conflict and grief I have seen is a result of some form of misunderstanding and lack of effective communication. So from this point on, you need to increase your awareness of other people's feelings. Do your best to understand them better, and before you express yourself, stop for a moment and imagine how you would feel if someone would tell you those exact words that are running on your mind. This simple step is the key to mindful communication.

Mindful Communication

Step 1.

Become aware the moment you are about to say something bad and insulting about someone.

Step 2.

Think about how you would feel if someone would tell you those exact words you are thinking.

Step 3.

Take three deep breaths and repeat the word "Clear" every time you exhale.

Step 4.

Think of someone that makes you happy. Imagine that the person is actually telling you to be nice.

Step 5.

Think of something positive to say. Instead of saying something bad or mean about someone, give them a nice complement about his or her clothes, shoes, watch, etc.

Step 6.

Repeat this steps as many times as possible to avoid expressing yourself in a negative way.

Step 7.

If all else fails, just walk away and don't say anything.

Our Behaviour

"Realizing that our actions, feelings and behaviours are the result of our own images and beliefs gives us the level that psychology has always needed for changing personality."
- Maxwell Maltz

Have you ever heard the song "You make your own heaven or hell right here on earth" by the Temptations? If you pay attention to the lyrics, you can really appreciate the brilliant message behind the song. It is true, you create your own heaven or hell in your life; remember when you were young and life seemed so simple; however, as you got older life became more complex and complicated. In reality, life is simple but as adults we over complicate our lives in almost every aspect. The famous Irish writer and poet Oscar Wilde expressed this perfectly.

> *Life is not complex. We are complex.*
> *Life is simple and the simple thing is the right thing.*
> *- Oscar Wilde*

People for some reason or another tend to find ways to make things just a bit more complicated; notice that I wrote "people find." That's right, everyone is responsible for the lifestyle they live and this includes you. Remember if you take credit for your accomplishments, you also have to take credit for your failures. If you blame others for what is going on in your life (positive or negative), you're denying responsibility, and ultimately you are giving up control over that part of your life.

Sometimes I'm amazed how complicated the life of some of my clients are the first time I see them. They come in to the office with two smart phones, a laptop, a tablet, a smartwatch and a mp3 player. They have countless appointments, work eighty hours a week and spend most of their free time on Facebook, Twitter and other social networking sites. With all this technology you would think that they would have no problem communicating with people but one of the most common issues that I come across in my practice is the sense of not being able to connect with others. In these cases my job as a coach is to let my clients remember that life is not that complicated, that they have the solution to make life simple again.

Our Behaviour

All you have to remember is what's important in life, to be yourself and focus on quality instead of quantity. This applies in every aspect of your life: career, experiences, possessions, relationships, etc. Start connecting with everything and everyone in a deeper level; stop doing things just for the sake of doing something. Stop surrounding yourself with people just for the sake of not being alone. Stop buying things just because you can. It is not about the quantity, it is all about the quality.

Here is the key to happiness: Fill yourself with love, respect and knowledge. For, you see, first you have to love yourself, respect yourself, and know yourself before you can share these qualities with others. If you choose to fill yourself with hate, rejection, and ignorance; that is all you'll be able to share and that is all the world will be able to share with you. "You make your own heaven or hell right here on earth." Does it start to make more sense now?

Let me share a story that dramatically depicts the difference between heaven and hell, told by my professor Flavio Souza Ph.D. during one of his brilliant lectures.

A man spoke with an angel. The man wished more than anything to see for himself the difference between heaven and hell, "Come, I will show you hell" said the angel.

They entered a room where a large group of people sat around a huge feast of food. All the food looked fresh and succulent. However, everyone in this place looked famished, desperate and starved. Each held a spoon that reached the food, but each spoon had a handle much longer than their own arm, so it could not be used to get the food into their own mouths. The man heard their desperate weeping and moaning. The suffering was terrible and the man cried "I've seen enough, please let me see heaven."

"Come, now I will show you heaven," the angel said. They entered another room, identical to the first. The succulent feast, a group of people, the same long spoons. But in this room everyone was happy and well-nourished. The man was confused "I don't understand," said the man. "Why are they so happy here when they were miserable in the other room and everything is the same?"

The angel smiled, "It is simple, look closer" he said. As the man looked closer, he noticed laughter filled the air as the people in heaven were using those long spoons to feed each other.

It is a beautiful story that highlights the foundation to true happiness in life; to give and receive, to care for the wellbeing of others as they do for you. In the story everyone in heaven was an infant and a parent at the same time, feeding and being fed; the most powerful bond possible. It is time for you to simplify your life, to experience passion in everything you do and to share your success. This will fill your life with peace, enjoyment and satisfaction.

Allow me to raise another important point regarding treating other people with dignity. Have you ever heard or read about the Milgram experiment on obedience? You can watch Stanley Milgram's famous experiment on YouTube or any other video-sharing website. By the way, you don't have to be a psychologist or psychiatrist to understand the implications this experiment revealed. I will give you a brief description of the set-up and the results of the experiment, since I only want to make a point on the way some people behave under certain circumstances.

The participants were average ordinary people that thought they were involved in a learning experiment. They were told that during the experiment they would have the roll of the teacher and another person of the learner. The "teacher" would sit in front of a shock generator and he was ordered by an individual in a lab coat to deliver an ever increasing electrical shock to the "learner," every time he gave a wrong answer. The "teacher" was not actually delivering an electrical shock. The "learner" in the experiment was an actor in another room; however the participant "the teacher" could clearly hear the screams of pain every time they supposedly delivered the electrical shocks.

As you can imagine the results were shocking. All the participant actually followed the order to administer the supposedly electrical shock. Sixty-five percent followed orders to the extent of endangering the life of the "learner" (another human being). Of course Milgram's experiment was conducted in a laboratory setting, so you might make the case that it doesn't quite apply to "real life." After all who is going to ask you to deliver a dangerous electrical shock to another human being.

My point is that we should reject any urge, suggestion or command to inflict any kind of harm to another human being. Would you refuse to deliver even the weakest electrical shock or would you follow the orders from the authority figure? I am pretty sure we all like to believe we would do the right thing under the same circumstances. I also understand that everyone is constantly required to behave in a specific way under particular environments and situations but always remember "Do to others as you would have them do to you."

Remember to always give people your undivided attention. It makes them feel appreciated, interesting, and respected. You will be surprised how ordinary interaction flows in a deeper level when you make an effort to connect with others. Follow the steps on the following exercise to connect with people in the deeper level.

Connect With Others

Step 1.

Always remember that a picture is worth a thousand words, so the picture of yourself that you present to others is worth a thousand words in their minds; so strive to make a good impression on people, especially if it is a first impression.

Step 2.

Adopt the mirroring technique to quickly create the kind of emotional attraction that will make people want to connect with you on a deeper level.

Step 3.

Pay attention to the person you are interacting with. Discreetly match his/her body language; mirror his/her posture and body movements. Wait about 10 seconds, and then shift your body in the same way they did. Use the same hand gestures he/she uses, but only when it's your turn to talk.

Step 4.

Match their tonality; you'll want to talk at their volume during the whole conversation. Listen to how they pronounce their words and match them.

Step 5.

Follow their speech tempo. If he/she talks slowly, then you talk slowly; if they talk fast, then you talk fast.

Step 6.

To establish a connection to the deepest level; pay close attention to their language and match it using the same words they use. For example if he/she says "I *see* what you mean" then your reply should be "That is the way I *see* it". If they say "It doesn't *sound* right to me" then your reply should be "It *sounds* like you really understand the issue". If they say "I like the way you *handled* yourself," your response should be "That is the way it needed to be *handled*".

Step 7.

Mastering the mirroring technique require an effort of the will. You may not be entirely successful to establish a deeper connection at first, but keep practicing and you will succeed.

Part Four
Manifesting Your Goals

Imagination

"Magic mirror on the wall. Who is the fairest of them all?"
- Evil Queen by the Brothers Grimm

Did you know that imagination will defeat will power any day, under any circumstance? It is true, you can have all the will power you want to achieve a specific goal but if you have a different plan at the unconscious level, your subconscious mind will use the power of your imagination to sabotage your plan and believe me it will.

If you don't believe me, let me share two examples: Lets say you want to lose some weight. Consciously you make an effort to buy healthy food and even sign up at the local fitness center. You feel proud of yourself for taking this mindful steps toward healthy living. On your first day of your diet you wake up earlier to prepare a healthy lunch to take to work. At lunch time you finish eating your meal. All of the sudden you start craving something sweet, maybe a large slice of apple pie or a moist slice of chocolate cake. Your subconscious mind starts sending images of that delicious slice of cake or pie. You can imagine biting into it and tasting the rich sweetness, you can even smell it. You try to put it out of your mind but the picture, taste and smell keep coming back. You suppress the feeling for the rest of the afternoon by keeping busy at work.

When you leave work, you head down to the fitness center. You exercise for an hour and when you finish your workout you are feeling great. When you get home you are ready for a healthy meal, after all your body is demanding nutrients since it just burned all that energy during your exercise routine. You prepare your meal and sit down to eat it. After dinner all of a sudden the image of that slice of cake or pie "pops" back into your mind. You might have enough will power to suppress it for the time being. This scenario is repeated for a couple of days. After a couple of days your imagination gets the better of you and it becomes too much work to suppress that image of the cake. When you go grocery shopping, "it just happened" that you walked by the bakery department and you see the deli-

Imagination

cious cake you've been craving. You tell yourself "just this once, I will stop after this one" and as we say, the rest is history. Your imagination just demonstrated who is in charge.

Let's take a look at another example: Let's say you are a smoker and you want to quit (if you don't smoke, good for you). You know you can do it, you are determined, after all your will power is strong. You smoked your last cigarette and you are done with the old habit. You feel proud of yourself. You get up in the morning and get ready to go to work. By the time you get to your car, you're already craving to smoke but you make a great effort not to smoke. You jump right into your duties at work to keep your mind busy. Around lunch time your subconscious mind starts sending images of a lit up cigarette. You are feeling unconformable, so you head down to the snack machine to easy the discomfort. After lunch your subconscious once again start sending images, taste, and even the smell of cigarettes. So once again you head down to the snack machine. After work you run into one of smoking buddies. The smell of the cigarettes if too much, your will power weakens and your imagination places the nail in the coffin by compounding images, taste and feelings, game over. Your imagination once again beats your will power hands down.

It is very important that you remember the following:

Your will power is run by your conscious mind, and your imagination is powered by your subconscious mind. You might make a decision consciously, but the subconscious mind may have a different program running. If you want to make a permanent change, you need to have both the conscious mind and the subconscious mind working together.

I don't want you to worry believing that imagination is all bad. On the contrary, imagination is the source of all good. Have you ever talked to a child? They can imagine a perfect world, a land where everyone is safe and happy. It is imagination that allows every child to grow into a strong and productive human being. A parent can very easily tap and connect with their child by stepping into their imaginary world. This process can create a bond that will last a life time; the power of imagination can literally bring people together.

Imagination allows any human being of any age to expand his or her horizon on any field or area of interest such as musical, social, linguistic, academic, or in relationships. The fact is that imagination is essential to the mental health of the entire society. Any inventor or scientist will tell you this; without it, all creation of alternative solutions will interrupt the forward movement of a nation, bringing it down to it's knees. Can you imagine what our world would look like without the imagination of great historical figures like Leonardo Da Vinci, Benjamin Franklin, Nikola Tesla, Henry Ford, or Albert Einstein? We probably would still be riding horses and lighting a candle in the middle of the night.

Believe me when I tell you this: if you are facing a crisis in your life, it is not because the economy, your level of education or even your social status. It is because you are lacking imagination; It is because you cannot imagine your life being any different from where you are now. If you feel stuck or maybe you feel like your life is going nowhere, it is because you actually have learned how to dismiss your imagination. You see, imagination is a trait that we humans are born with it. It doesn't matter from which socio-economic background a child is from, you will always find them fantasizing in one way or another, always doing her/his best to enjoy life. I bet as a child no one ever taught you how to have fun using your imagination, you just did it. In fact people (adults) probably had to stop you from utilizing your imagination, from having fun.

Imagination

So if you're struggling to achieve a certain goal or trying to overcome a physical disability, but somehow you're still not getting results, use your imagination. Using your imagination can help you find a solution. It will make you move forward, both physically and mentally. I know it sounds cliché but apply the old philosophy "Think outside of the box". All men and women throughout history have overcome huge obstacles using their imaginations. In the clinical world researchers have discovered that the power of imagination has been validated as a way to reduce the intensity of patient's pain, to alleviate their anxiety and even to decrease the amount of pain medication they need.

Let me give you this suggestion: "Let your imagination soar"

Let Your Imagination Guide You

Step 1.

Find a moment each day to start utilizing your imagination to find the answers you are searching for or to achieve the goals you want to achieve.

Step 2.

Find a place at home or at work where you can sit down and imagine that you can be transported to a fun place. This place can be a place you create or a physical place you had fun when you were younger. (If you have children and can't be by yourself, don't worry. Share the experience and enjoy this place together).

Step 3.

Imagine walking around in this place. Notice all the details of the landscape, hear all the sounds, connect with all those feelings of joy.

Step 4.

Allow yourself to be completely free in this place. This is your world. If you want to fly, then fly. If you want to swim with the dolphins, then imagine becoming a dolphin. Free yourself during this experience.

Step 5.

See the world through a different angle and give yourself permission to laugh, have fun and be free.

Step 6.

Notice the different feelings you are experiencing. Imagine that you can take control of those feelings and start spinning them in any direction around your body. The faster you spin them the stronger they become.

Step 7.

Now think of a time in the future where you are applying these great feelings. See and feel yourself taking steps that will actually direct you toward your goal. In the following days after this exercise, notice what resources and answers your subconscious mind brings forward. Repeat this exercise every time you are searching for an answer or just want to feel better.

Visualization

"Visualize this thing that you want, see it, feel it, believe in it. Make your mental blue print, and begin to build."
- Robert Collier

People often ask me what is the difference between visualization and imagination; the interpretation seems to get some people confused and others believing is the same thing. You can search online for the definition for both and you probably will get several different descriptions. So, allow me to share with you an analogy that my late professor and spiritual guide Santiago Aranegui shared with his whole class.

Just picture yourself driving home from work. You are listening to the radio but not really paying attention. At certain point you begin to *imagine* what you are going to do when you get home. You know you will prepare something to eat but you don't know exactly what. You know you will watch something on TV but you are not sure what exactly. If you have children you know you will interact with them but you don't exactly know how. All this is happening while you are still driving, listening to the radio and maybe even talking on the phone. So as you can see imagination can be very vague.

On the other hand, if you were driving home from work and you wanted to visualize what you are going to do when you get there, you will first have to pull over. Otherwise you will have an accident. Park on a safe place, shift the gear to park, turn off the radio and silence your phone; then you will have to clear your mind and start actually visualizing with great detail every step you will perform the moment you pull into the drive way. You also will have to pay attention to all the feelings you will experience with every action you take. For example, if you have children, you will visualize how you will greet them and how you will feel when you see them or hug them (happiness, joy, etc.). If you are going to cook, you have to visualize every step, from preparing the food, the smell and even the tasting of it. Once you are done with your visualization you can once again continue driving.

Visualization

Let me explain, visualization needs your full attention because you will be creating images in your mind towards a specific goal, producing an actual physical sensation. In other words is the *concentration* and the *intent* that determines the difference between *visualization* and *imagination*.

If the common saying "seeing is believing," then visualization is truly the most powerful tool at your disposal. It is no wonder that just about every professional athlete in every sports practices visualization to enhance their performance. Artists from every community visualize their art work before bringing it to life; inventors harness the power of visualization before even making a prototype. If your mind can see it, hear it, smell it, taste it or feel it, then the mind makes it real.

Have you ever experienced hypnosis? I know, I know; isn't that what those mysterious performers on stage command a group of people to do weird things like bark like a dog or take their clothes off? You might ask. Yes, that is one type of hypnosis; what we call Stage hypnosis. However, I'm referring to hypnotherapy (Therapy that is undertaken with a subject under hypnosis.)

Before I dive into the subject of hypnosis, let me clear out some common misconceptions about hypnosis that you might have heard, seen or read about.

Hypnosis is not safe: That is utterly false. Hypnosis is a normal state of consciousness. Everyone experiences hypnotic states several times each day, while driving, while watching TV, while reading a book or daydreaming.

People lose consciousness and have amnesia: A hypnotized subject is never unconscious. They often have their eyes closed and are deeply relaxed, so they look asleep but in fact, the subjects are remarkably alert and focused. It is true that a small percentage of people experience amnesia after a hypnotic session. But unless it's suggested, hypnosis does not create any form of amnesia.

People reveal deep personal secrets: False; under hypnosis a person will not reveal any intimate secrets he/she would not tell while in a wakeful state.

Only gullible or weak minded people can be hypnotized: Being hypnotized is not an indication of lesser intelligence. Quite the opposite, hypnosis requires the ability to focus and concentrate; which means the more intelligent you are, the more likely you are to be successful with hypnosis.

Fear of getting stuck in hypnosis: Once again this is completely false. Remember that you more aware during hypnosis than in your normal state of mind. Since the subject is in total control, there is no difficulty in emerging from a hypnotic state.

A hypnotized person can be made to do anything: Without sounding repetitive, the subject is always in control and will decide whether to cooperate or not. If a suggestion is ever given that the subject doesn't agree with, he/she will simply not follow it.

There is nothing mysterious, scary, or weird about hypnosis. As a matter of fact, hypnosis it is nothing out of the ordinary. Think of hypnosis as a goal oriented guided meditation or visualization process. This process takes advantage of the vast creative power of visualization to achieve effective results. In my practice, I utilize hypnosis for a wide range of issues such as weight loss, smoking cessation, relaxation, healing, pain management and stress relief, just to name a few. I also implement it to reach new desired goals or to get rid of undesired behaviours and beliefs.

Visualization

I am constantly encouraging people to experience hypnosis to improve their lives. It's no wonder that the implementation of hypnosis by mental health professionals has increased steadily in recent years. Hypnosis is gaining acceptance in conventional medicine as a safe, reliable, and effective alternative to other, more traditional methods. However, it is very important that you to choose your therapist carefully. Make sure that you hire a certified or licensed hypnotherapist that is well trained in hypnosis and knowledgeable relating to the issue you want to address.

Since hypnosis (guided visualization) is based on the concept that your mind and body are connected, it's very easy to understand how your mind and body respond as though what you are visualizing is real; that is the key to manifest what you desire. What is even more important to understand is the fact that you can perform hypnosis all by yourself; you don't need to be a trained hypnotherapist in order to effectively hypnotize yourself. It just takes a bit of effort and practice.

You can utilize self-hypnosis in order to stay happy, healthy and positive in your life. Integrate this powerful tool to tap into the potential that lays within you; believe me when I tell you the following: *If you practice self-hypnosis regularly, things in your life will change for the better.*

Self Hypnosis

Step 1.

Before starting this self hypnosis exercise, select a spot where you will not be disturbed for about 30 minutes. Sit in any comfortable chair or couch. Take three deep easy breaths to relax yourself. As you inhale, feel the fresh, relaxing air entering your body. When you exhale, feel any tension, worries or negativity leaving your body.

Step 2.

Continue to relax, breathing easily and naturally. Close your eyes and repeat the word "Relax" every time you exhale. Repeat this until you have done it twelve times. Imagine each part of your body becoming lighter and lighter as the tension is removed. Relax your feet, slowly relax your calves, thighs, hips, stomach, lower back, chest, shoulders, arms, hands, fingers, upper back, neck, face and head, until you've relaxed your whole body.

Step 3.

Continue breathing easily and naturally. Imagine you are at the top of a flight of seven stairs. Visualize every detail of this scene from the top to the bottom. Tell yourself that you are going to descend the stairs, counting each step down, starting at seven. Picture each number in your mind. Imagine that each number you count is further down and one step closer to the bottom. After each number, you will feel yourself drifting deeper and deeper into a profound relaxation.

Visualization

Step 4.

At the bottom of the steps you should feel completely relaxed. Once you have achieved this state, you should proceed in stating your purpose (Decide upon what it is you want). Mentally start to narrate what you are doing and think in the present and future tense.

Step 5.

Visualize three doors in front of you and imagine that through these doors are the answers to your purpose. Once you can clearly see the doors, open them slowly one at a time and describe to yourself what is happening when you open each one. Allow your subconscious mind to bring forth any information, don't over think or rationalize things. If you see an image, a symbol or hear anything internally, keep it in mind. If for any reason you don't understand the meaning of it, ask your subconscious for the meaning.

Step 6.

Once you are satisfied with what you have done, go back to the stairs and start going back up, feel with each step you take. You're becoming lighter and lighter until you have once again reached that first step.

Step 7.

Once you have ascended, give yourself a few moments before opening your eyes. When you have opened your eyes. Tell yourself "Awake and aware, Awake and aware, Awake and aware." This will put your mind back in the conscious state.

* Self hypnosis requires an effort of the will and you may not be entirely successful at first, but keep practicing and you will succeed.

Meditation

"Meditation brings wisdom; lack of mediation leaves ignorance. Know well what leads you forward and what holds you back and choose the path that leads to wisdom."
- Buddha Gautama Siddharta

I clearly remember the morning of November 9th of 2011. After my morning routine, I got on the computer and checked my email. The subject in one of the hundreds of spam emails called my attention. The heading read "Street Darma: Teaching Meditation to the Homeless," the article was in the Huffington Post and it was written by BJ Gallangher. The article described how a man named Keiley Jon Clark teaches meditation to homeless in San Antonio, Texas. It was an incredible article and I was moved by the kindness and effort Mr. Clark practice to help the less fortunate. Through meditation Mr. Clark helps every person that wants to break old thought patterns and behaviours.

I cannot emphasize this enough: "Meditate," let me repeat that again "Meditate," one more time so it can sink in "Meditate." In this chapter, I am going to do my best to convince you to meditate on a daily base. I promise you, if you meditate, your life will be more meaningful, a lot of things that before were not clear, all of the sudden will make sense. In other words, your life will become "Magic."

If you want to mentally go to a quiet place, without all the clutter in the mind or be in the moment and have more clarity, lucidity, and be more focused in your thinking, meditation is the answer. Meditation merges your mind and body to help you be more centered and relaxed during your every day life. Practicing meditation opens the door to understanding, it awakens your consciousness.

Imagine you are stepping into a house that is full of clutter, garbage and junk, loud music blasting from the speakers on a music system, three flat screens showing different shows with the volume turned all the way up, and the smoke alarm going off; not a pleasant place. Well, that is exactly what goes on in your head if you are not in control of your mind. The house is your mind, the clutter are your thoughts, the loud music is you inner dialogue, the shows in the flat screens are all those pictures and movies you keep running in your head and the smoke alarm going off is something that is causing you stress. Now imagine that progressively, little by little, you start to clear some of the clutter, turn down the volume on the music system, then turn off the flat screens; that is exactly what meditation does. All of the sudden you start to find some answers among the cleared space, you also will find new room to place more useful and practical items in this new found space.

Meditation is a very simple process that anybody can fit into their busy daily schedule. Unfortunately most people today don't take the time to practice this easy process that can improve our lives in so many ways. Allow me to describe very briefly several different types of meditation:

The term meditation is derived from the Latin word meditari, meaning "to contemplate or to think." So the word meditation conveys different meanings from person to person, depending on the culture setting. But for the purpose of simplicity, the different types of meditation I will outline here are some of the more popular in the western society. There are many types of meditations techniques, but they all share the same goal "to achieve inner peace".

Ways to meditate:

• *Guided Meditation*: This method of meditation produces mental images or movies of places, situations and symbols you find relaxing. Guided meditation is intended to be a journey where the imagination is lead by an outside source, for the purpose of relaxation or solving an issue. You may be guided through this process by a hypnotherapist, teacher or a recording.

- *Mantra Meditation*: In Hinduism the word Mantra means "sacred word or prayer." During Mantra meditation, you'll repeat silently or out loud a calming word or phrase. The goal is to be in harmony with the higher self, a sort of self-awakening or transformation.

- *Mindfulness Meditation*: Just like the name implies, this type of meditation is all about focusing on being aware of your thoughts and actions in the present moment without any judgement. You pay attention to what you are experiencing during meditation, for example: the sound of your breath.

- *Tai chi*: Tai Chi can be translated as the "Supreme Ultimate Force" and is often associated with the Chinese concept of yin-yang. It is a form of gentle Chinese martial arts emphasizing on complete relaxation, and is essentially a form of meditation.

- *Transcendental meditation:* In this type of meditation you use a mantra to decrease your conscious awareness and eliminate all thoughts from your mind. The ultimate goal in practicing Transcendental Meditation is to achieve a state of perfect stillness and consciousness.

- *Yoga*. The word Yoga comes from the Sanskrit word "Yuj" meaning to yoke or unite. During the process of Yoga you perform a series of postures and controlled breathing exercises to promote a more balanced and useful life. While moving through poses that require balance and concentration, you are encouraged to focus on the moment.

With meditation you can learn to implement the power of the mind. This simple process allows you to tune in with an infinite number of memories, feelings, knowledge and resources. Meditation puts you in touch with your higher self and it can make you the ruler of your own destiny.

Meditation

If the ultimate goal for humanity is to achieve a perfect balance between mind, body and spirit; then meditation is the key. The more you understand the connection, dynamics and components between the mind, the body and the soul, the more complete health and balance you will bring to your life.

Did you know that your body is designed to release 60% of its toxins through breathing? That is a fact. Breathing releases tension and can help with pain relief. When you start meditating, always be aware of your breathing. In order to breathe properly while meditating you need to breathe deeply into your abdomen not just your chest, you should take deep, slow, rhythmic breaths through the nose, not through the mouth.

The most important things of all before, during, and after meditation, to always *enjoy yourself*.

Meditation

Step 1.

First thing in the morning: Find a comfortable spot. Somewhere you won't be disturbed for 15 minutes. Sit on a straight back chair and allow your hands to lie relaxed in your lap, your knees should not touch each other. Separate your feet but keep them placed firmly on the floor. When you are finally relaxed, close your eyes and take a deep breath, hold it for a count of seven and then release it easily. Repeat this, taking another deep breath and holding it for the count of seven. Then rest and repeat this until you have done it seven times.

Step 2.

Continue to relax, breathing naturally. With your eyes closed think of the color green, any shade of green from light green to a deep green. Think of just one shade during a meditation period. Feel it all around you. Fill the entire room with this color. Do this for one minute, do not let your mind wander.

Step 3.

As you continue to relax in the same position. Think of a piano, or any musical instrument you are familiar with playing a relaxing song. Carry this tune in your mind for a minute, do not let your mind wander, then turn it off. After a minute let go and continue to relax.

Step 4.

Continue to relax in the same position. Focus your attention on the top of your head. Your mind creates all the emotions you experience. Feel your mind creating emotions of relaxation, concentration, and peace. All these feelings of relaxation, concentration, and peace take the form of a thick white liquid.

Step 5.

Now imagine and feel that this thick white liquid will spread slowly all over your body from the top of your head all the way down to your toes and it will saturate every muscle, every fiber, every cell in your body with relaxation, concentration, and peace.

Step 6.

Take seven deep breath and repeat the word "Relax" every time you exhale. Continue to relax, breathing easily and naturally. Allow your mind to achieve a state of perfect stillness for the next five minutes.

Step 7.

Remain calm in the same position. With your eyes closed, mentally repeat the follow affirmations three times each (one affirmation per each breath):

"Today is the best day of my life."

"Everyday, in every way, I am getting better and better."

"Every cell in my body vibrates with relaxation, concentration, and peace."

Take three deep breaths. Open you eyes, take notice how relaxed you feel. Repeat this meditation exercise every day.

Part Five
Ignorance Is Not Bliss

Energy

"Energy and persistence conquer all things."
- Benjamin Franklin

We are dual beings. You might not realize how powerful that statement is, but I will explain very clearly the concept behind it, so you can be more aware how everything that surrounds you has a positive or negative effect in your life.

Just about everyone knows that everything in the universe is essentially made up of two things: matter and energy. Of course matter is all the physical things like your body, our planet, the starts, this book, etc. On the other hand, energy is what animates matter and it is in constant motion or vibration, for example: Plants use light (energy) from the sun to grow; we use energy to make heat or to move things.

To make things a little bit clearer let me illustrate another example: water; in nature water can be found in three fundamental states of matter: liquid, solid, and gas. Water in liquid form has a certain vibratory rate (energy), if you slow the amount of vibration the water turns into ice; if you raise the amount of vibration it turns into gas (very simplistic explanation). The point is: just like matter, energy is all around us.

In chapter seventeen you will learn more about the Seven Universal Laws; one of these universal laws "The Law of Vibration" states that everything in the universe moves and vibrates, meaning that everything is made out of energy. In other words we are living in an ocean of energy. This same universal law declares that the energy that we send out we attack. This is the source of the now well known Law of Attraction.

Since we are living in an ocean of energy, it is very easy to understand that your thoughts and emotions are energy too; what this means is that every aspect of your life depends on the direction and the amount of energy you are willing to employ. Every thought, emotion, feeling, and action is energy flowing throughout the physical universe (matter).

Energy

It is for this reason that it is necessary to pay attention to your energy flow; there are many ways that you can store and lose energy, for example: you walk into a meeting with your boss, colleagues or friends. After a short period of time you sense a negative atmosphere (energy). How do you think you will feel by the end of this meeting? I am willing to bet you probably will be completely drained and disheartened.

It is essential that you boost your energy levels by exercising, meditating, eating healthy and resting properly. The choice is yours, you either take care of yourself to harness energy or live on empty which makes life much harder. In the Hindu tradition we learn about the energy centers called Chakras. The chakras are vortexes of energy vertically located from the crown of your head to the base of your spine. Of course Chakras are not physical organs, they are part of your energy or etheric body. It is believed that through these energy centers we receive, store and supply energy. The Chakras are associated with your physical, mental, and spiritual well-being. According to the tradition, if the chakras are not balanced, energy will be blocked; therefore depending on which Chakra is blocked, you would feel either a physical or psychological dysfunction.

It is a well-know fact that energy healing or energy therapy brings about documented cures. Today energy healing is considered alternative or integrative medicine and is widely accepted as an effective method for restoring mind and body to a balanced state. There are numerous amounts of therapies under the umbrella of energy medicine, so I will briefly touch upon the better well known; but before I do, I would like to clarify that energy healing does not replace conventional medicine and it should not be used as an alternative to seeking medical advice.

Acupuncture: Chinese medicine defines acupuncture as a technique for balancing the flow of energy known as Qi or Chi

(Chee). The energy or Qi flows through energy channels or meridians. When the flow of energy is disturbed, disease is likely to occur. According to acupuncture practitioners, inserting needles into specific points along these meridians causes blocked energy to be released and the system to be restored into balance. Acupuncture can successfully treat a wide range of conditions including: muscle and nerve pain, earache, high blood pressure, food allergies, premenstrual syndrome, chronic fatigue, and stress. (This is by not a complete list of what acupuncture can treat.) Acupuncture is often used as a preventative medicine.

Reiki: Reiki is a type of energy therapy that centers on the manipulation of Ki (energy), the Japanese version of Qi. Reiki healing is purely based on balancing the flow of energy in the person; the same concept as acupuncture in traditional Chinese medicine. To me, one of the most touching aspect regarding Reiki healers is their great disposition to help others without expecting anything in return. Most of the time these wonderful people would offer a weekly or monthly free Reiki Healing Circle to help their fellow human beings who may be ill or working with particularly challenging situations. I have seen them performing Reiki for AIDS patients, senior citizens, people with addiction and other serious health issues without taking a single dime. These are some of the benefits of Reiki: release stress and tension, better sleep, reduces blood pressure, relieve headaches, and increases energy levels. (This is not a complete list of all the benefits Reiki can provide).

Qigong: The word Qigong is made up of two Chinese words Qi and Gong. Qi as you know means energy and Gong means accomplishment or cultivation; so together Qigong means Energy Cultivation. The practice of Qigong involves posture, breathing techniques, and mental focus to cleanse, increase, and heal the body. People that consistently practice Qigong declare that it helps them regain a youthful energy, maintain good health and it helps them recover from illness faster. These are some of the benefits of Qigong: increased energy, relaxes mind and body, promotes a healthy sleep, it helps the body eliminate toxins, clears the skin, improves digestion, creates a peaceful approach to life. (This is not a complete list of all the benefits Qigong can provide).

There are other types of energy therapy, including: mesmerism, magnet therapy, light therapy, crystal healing, reconnective healing and many more. In the past all these effective and helpful forms of energy medicine were frowned upon, but today with more scientific studies backing up the claims of so many people in the public, it has begun to attract more widespread interest.

Follow the steps on the following exercise to increase your physical, mental and spiritual level of energy.

The following exercise targets only the four higher energy centers since the lower three already receive too much attention through out our life. We have to develop the higher energy centers to become balanced in our lives.

Create Positive Energy

Step 1.

First thing in the morning: find a comfortable spot. Somewhere you won't be disturbed for thirty minutes. Sit on a straight back chair and allow your hands to lie relaxed in your lap, your knees should not touch each other. Separate your feet but keep them placed firmly on the floor. When you are finally relaxed, close your eyes and take a three deep breaths.

Step 2.

Continue to relax, breathing naturally. With your eyes closed concentrate and visualize a circle of White light in the crown of your head. Imagine that this circle of light starts to spin faster and faster, creating an energy of peace and calmness; with every breath you take, feel the circle spinning faster and faster, the sense of peace becoming greater and greater. After you achieve a complete feeling of peace, take a deep breath and release that visualization, put it completely out of your mind.

Step 3.

As you continue to relax in the same position, concentrate and visualize a circle of Purple light in the middle your forehead. Imagine that this circle of light starts to spin faster and faster, creating an energy of motivation and vision; with every breath you take feel the circle spinning faster and faster and the sense of motivation becoming greater and greater. After you achieve the level of motivation you desire, take a deep breath and release that visualization, put it completely out of your mind.

Step 4.

Continue to relax in the same position. Concentrate and visualize a circle of Blue light in your throat. Imagine that this circle of light starts to spin faster and faster, creating an energy and a sense of trust and compassion; with every breath you take feel the circle spinning faster and faster, and the sense of trust becoming greater and greater. After you achieve a complete feeling of trust, take a deep breath and release that visualization, put it completely out of your mind.

Step 5.

Continue to relax in the same position. Concentrate and visualize a circle of Green light in your heart. Imagine that this circle of light starts to spin faster and faster, creating an energy and a sense of love and sincerity; with every breath you take feel the circle spinning faster and faster and the sense of love becoming greater and greater. After you achieve the level of love and sincerity you desire, take a deep breath and release that visualization, put it completely out of your mind.

Step 6.

Continue to relax in the same position. If you wish to share this positive energy you are experiencing with someone; visualize that person or group of people clearly. See he/she/them surrounded by a white light. Feel the love for this person as you share the energy.

Step 7.

Remain calm in the same position. Take three deep breaths. Open you eyes, take notice how relaxed you feel. Repeat this exercise once a week.

Frequency

"Everything in the universe resonates with a particular frequency, from a single thought to a simple sound wave, everything has a frequency"
- Flavio S. Campos

Have you ever walked into a home or a business and felt it had "bad vibes?" Or maybe met someone without even knowing them and just felt like they had bad intentions or "bad vibes"? You might not realize it but what you are actually feeling is the frequencies that your nervous system is sensing and your subconscious mind is registering. The analytical conscious mind most of the time cannot comprehend what the subconscious mind is communicating and this is for a good reason; if we would be able to interpret and register all these frequencies consciously we would go insane, there is just too much information to process.

Let me give you an example to demonstrate how important frequencies are. Imagine that you have two tuning forks (two-pronged(tines) U-shaped metal device) mounted in a sound box on your dinning table. Now imagine that you strike the first tuning fork and the tines begin vibrating. Of course you can hear the sound; next you grab the tines of the tuning fork you struck to prevent from vibrating; surprisingly, you still can hear the sound, why? Because now the sound is being produced by the second tuning fork, the one which you didn't strike. This is call resonance.

In this example you can really appreciate how one tuning fork forces another tuning fork into the same vibrational motion. Why is this so important? Well, the same happens to you and every human being in the world; everyone is influenced by the frequency around them. You could actually say that we vibrate at our own different frequencies but are heavily influenced by the environment we find ourselves in.

This is why it is so crucial to choose your company and living environment wisely. You are probably familiar with the old expression "Tell me who your friends are and I'll tell you who you are." This is a great expression that explains the power of frequency or resonance. I know that most of us would like to believe that we are completely free from the influences of the world around us. After all you are in charge of how you feel and nobody tells you what to do or how to feel, right? The fact is that you are responsible for your actions but it is very important to identify what or who is influencing you.

Have you ever heard of the term Social Proof? Social proof is a type of compliance; you know those times when you weren't sure what to do during a social situation and you looked around at other people to decide what to do; that is Social Proof and it doesn't matter how independent you might think you are. It is always a factor because it works on the subconscious level. So why do I bring this up? To urge you to look at the people and environment around you; I want you to observe the people you come in constant contact with in your life. Do they behave in a considerate manner towards you and others? If they lack integrity maybe it is time to start distancing yourself from them and start making new acquaintances.

I understand that no one is perfect but it is important that you start setting some boundaries. Remember that in one way or another they are influencing you, always keep that in mind. Let me give you an example: Let's say you're trying to make a change in your life, naturally you will most likely have doubts; if you are surrounded by negative people, they certainly will make those doubts a hundred times bigger. They will provide negative feedback; make you second guess yourself; cloud your judgement and make you feel terrible if things don't go as planned. In most cases this doesn't mean they don't care about you, they just don't want to see you get hurt.

Understandably it can be very difficult to control who you come into contact with throughout the day. For example dealing with negativity at home can be extremely difficult because these are the people you care for and love, you really don't want to distance yourself from them. So it is up to you to do your best to stay positive and to promote a positive attitude as an example for them to follow.

I don't want you to believe that what we consider negative is all bad. The truth is that whatever we perceive as negative in essence, brings us growth and learning. Let me share a metaphor to explain this point: Imagine that you go to the gym on a regular basis; you want to tone and grow muscle, so you lift weights; you use the weights as a resistance to make your muscles grow. So, in reality negativity is just like the weights, they make us grow. But this doesn't mean you should look for everything that is negative for the sake of growth, it doesn't work that way.

Remember that every aspect of your life is in resonance with the frequency that surrounds you. So how do you identify the frequency around you? It is very easy, examine the situations of your present life: health, relationships, living environment, career, financial, personal growth, and spirituality. Once you have assessed your life in all these important areas, notice which part of your life you're not satisfied with; do your best to find the source of the problems. It could be that you are holding on or avoiding something; maybe someone is intentionally holding you back. In other words, whatever part of your life you are having trouble with; that is exactly where you need to make changes to fluctuate to a positive frequency. Once you find the source, make changes in these troubled areas, you will notice how things develop; everything all of a sudden seems to flow forward with ease.

So how do you change the frequency where you are having problems? Well, it might not be easy at first but if you follow the seven step below I can assure you that you will definitely make a frequency shift.

1. *Believe in yourself* - Believing in yourself is all about being 100% sure that you are going to accomplish whatever you set your mind to do.

2. *Believe that you deserve happiness* - If you understand that you have the option to be happy and that you should be happy, then you can achieve the life that you desire.

3. *Release everything that is negative* - Many people consciously or unconsciously store a lot of negative emotions of anger, fear, guilt, shame, regret, and other toxic feelings. If you do, it is time to let go; time to forgive yourself and others.

4. *Take time for yourself* - You might be spending too much time taking care of other people; you need to make time for yourself. Spending a few minutes each day thinking about the things that make you happy is a great way to release stress and to stay positive.

5. *Stay healthy* - Achieving and maintaining good health is a great way to attain a balanced lifestyle (positive frequency). Take care of yourself by eating healthy, exercising, meditating, and expanding or learning new skills.

6. *Positive Influence* - Do your best to surround yourself with positive people who inspire and energize you.

7. *Share with others* - This is the most important of all the steps you can take to make a positive change in your life. Sharing wealth, joy, and happiness is a great way to make other people happy and in doing so, you will make yourself happy as well.

Higher Frequency

The sound of Aum (pronounced Om) has always been practiced in yoga. Aum is a universal sound. When you are tuned perfectly, you will receive positive vibrations and you will be able to merge with higher wavelength frequency. The practice of Aum leads to excellent mental and physical health. For example: It has a calming effect on the nerves, it has positive effect lowering blood pressure, it helps in relaxation and concentration. When you create peace and harmony in your life, those feelings have a ripple effect which influence other people in a positive way.

Step 1.

Find a place where you will not be disturbed for about 7 minutes. Sit on a straight back chair. Close your eyes and take three deep easy breaths to relax yourself. Continue to relax, breathing easily and naturally.

Step 2.

Once you feel that you have reached a comfortable state of relaxation, keep your mind calm and clear.

Step 3.

Inhale deeply through your nose and hold it for a count of seven and then release it creating the sound of Aum on the exhalations for as long as possible.

Step 4.

Repeat this process two more times, taking deep breaths and hold it for the count of seven and every time creating the sound of Aum on the exhalations.

Step 5.

Feel that the frequency and vibrations created by the Aum sounds flowing throughout every single cell in your whole body.

Step 6.

Continue to relax with a calm state of mind. Take a moment to feel, hear and visualize yourself as a happy infant, a happy teenager and a happy person in the present.

Step 7.

Remain calm in the same position. Take three deep breaths. Open you eyes, take notice how relaxed you feel. Repeat this exercise every day.

Manifestation

"The highest manifestation of life consists in this: that a being governs its own actions."
- St. Thomas Aquinas

In my coaching practice I have noticed how my clients share one key element for manifesting their goals: perseverance. The fact is that some of my clients had to overcome huge obstacles in their lives. With coaching they realized that the true reward in accomplishing their goals was the fact that they overcame those challenges in their lives. In other words, it is not the destination but the journey that counts. There is a beautiful Chinese story that really draws the spirit of perseverance and hard work.

Once upon a time, there was an old man in China, who had two big mountains in front of his home and it was very inconvenient for his whole family to come and go. One day the old man called all his family together to talk about how to move the two mountains to another place. His children and grandchildren all agreed and answered "Tomorrow we shall start to work" but his wife felt it was too difficult to move a mountain and replied: "You are an old man, you cannot even move a small hill, not to mention the two high mountains. Even if you could, where would you dispose of the stones and dirt from these mountains?" So he decided the stones and dirt would be dumped into the Bohai Sea.

They began working the next day. Their only digging tools were hoes and baskets; they chipped the rocks and shoveled the soil, and carried them in baskets to the Bohai Sea. None of the hardships and difficulties could deter the brave family. They worked on those mountains every day.

One day, a wise man, upon seeing them attempting to move the mountains laughed at the old man and tried to stop him, saying: "You are old and you can barely climb to the mountain top, you will never finish what you started." The old man drew a deep sigh and replied: "You are wrong. Yes, I am old and I will soon be dead, but I have children and when my children are dead, my grandchildren will continue. Generation after generation my

Manifestation

family will grow, but the mountains won't grow higher. With such determination and hard work, it is possible to move these tall mountains." The wise man had no words to reply.

So the old man and his family continued with their work day after day and year after year, through hot Summers and cold Winters until one day, the heavens heard how hard the old man and his whole family were working and asked the mountain gods to move the mountains away.

It never fails, everyone who succeeds in achieving their goals has one thing in common, they never give up. You know very well that sometimes staying motivated to achieve your goals is not the easiest thing to do, it takes discipline. But it helps to remember that the point of achieving your personal goals is to improve your life. Be always aware that no matter what obstacles you foresee, if you stay committed to accomplish your goals, your inner-strength will always carry you through.

Allow me to share with you a personal experience where I could have very easily given up on a personal goal I wanted to achieve. Both my colleague and I had been working hard on a project for several months. We expected to get a positive response regarding a possible new business venture; we got everything ready and gave our proposal, but instead of hearing "Yes, we want to do business with you," we literally heard nothing. The next morning I woke up and started reflecting on this huge disappointment. I began to feel sad and even felt a bit of discouragement sneaking in. At that moment I stopped all the negative thoughts in my head, I walked to the bathroom mirror and told myself "Jose, if it's for you, it will happen and nobody can take it away from you; if it was not meant to be, it was not for you." Eventually we got a positive result with their main competitor and believe it or not, later on we got the response we were looking for from the original company.

Over the years I have achieved many of my personal and professional goals. Allow me to share the approach I have always used. I can assure you, it will help you achieve your goals as well. There are three steps:

!. Always Make a Plan: Start a *Goal Journal* to help focus on your goals. Start by writing your short term goals first. Begin with the goals you want to manifest within three months followed by goals you want to achieve within six month and last the goals you want to achieve within a year. In a different paper or page; write down your long term goals; start with the goals you want to manifest within three years, then the goals you want to manifest within five years; and last the goals you want to manifest within ten years; always remember to write down realistic goals in your plan.

2. Create New Patterns: Your life is the result of your long term behaviour patterns, what we commonly call "habits". So to improve your life you will have to be willing to change or break some of your current patterns. Now, creating change might take a bit of hard work. As you know most people oppose change because they want to maintain their current comfort; they don't want to take any risks because deep inside they are truly afraid and to a certain point is understandable. But remember that within you lies great potential; so don't fall into the "comfort trap." That trap is a dream killer and it leads to a ordinary and boring life.

3. Be Persistent: It is very seldom that somebody can achieve a major personal goal overnight; if you have in the past, good for you. The truth is that most people have to dedicate a great deal of time and effort before they reach their goals; that doesn't mean you should only plan easy short term goals. On the contrary; you want to believe with every fiber in your being that you can accomplish whatever your goals are. You need to develop a conduct of honouring the promises you make to yourself; take charge and responsibility for your achievements and be aware that if you fall along the way, just pick yourself up right back again. Failure is only if you stay down after you fall down.

There is nothing stopping you from manifesting your goal. Keep you eyes open for new opportunities that will allow you to grow. It might sound like a cliché but do your best to think outside the box. In fact step out of the box and crush it, you don't belong in a box. I want you to plant the following thought in the deepest level of your mind; close your eyes and repeat the following thought three times: *"Within me lies the greatest potential and strength to achieve whatever my heart desires."*

Manifesting Your Goals

Step 1.

First thing in the morning or before going to bed: Find a comfortable spot; somewhere you won't be disturbed for ten minutes. Sit in a straight back chair. Close your eyes and take three deep easy breaths to relax yourself. Continue to relax, breathing easily and naturally.

Step 2.

Once you feel that you have reached a comfortable state of relaxation, imagine you have actually achieved the greatest personal goal you desire. See, hear, and feel yourself fully enjoying your accomplishment.

Step 3.

Take control of that great feeling of accomplishment and increase it. Make the feeling stronger and more intense, allow it to spread throughout your whole body.

Step 4.

Once you have taken control of this wonderful feeling that is throughout your body; see it, hear it and feel. Visualize this feeling as a flow of energy that surrounds your whole body; it could be any color, any sound or feeling.

Step 5.

Now, imagine that you transfer this flowing energy in all the steps that you need to take to achieve this personal goal, starting from the first step all the way to the last.

Step 6.

Visualize transferring this energy to other projects that you are currently working on or planning to start soon.

Step 7.

In the next days and weeks, observe if you find it easy to take those steps that you visualized.

Part Six
The Truth And Nothing But The Truth

The Seven Universal Laws

"When the ears of the student are ready to hear, then cometh the lips to fill them with wisdom."
- Hermes Trismegistus

Nowadays just about everyone has heard of the Law of Attraction. After all there are countless books, websites, articles and even movies about this law or principle. However, what most people don't realize is the fact that the Law of Attraction is only one of the Seven Universal Laws.

In this chapter I would like to go briefly over these Seven Universal Laws by which everything in the universe is governed. After reading and understanding the information I'm providing, I highly recommend that you start your own research on the subject as well. Of course being a student of the esoteric philosophies I suggest you read The Kybalion. The Kybalion is at the top of the list to learn and understand the Seven Universal Laws. You should read this book before any other titles, since most books dealing with this type of ancient knowledge are based on the teachings of The Kybalion.

Have you ever heard the term "The best things in life are free"? Well that is a fact and without being disrespectful to anyone, I believe it should be added as one of the universal laws. So, by knowing that the best things in life are free, the universe has given us a priceless gift, The Kybalion* is now in the public domain and it can be downloaded online for free for the eyes of the student who is ready to learn.

I want you to keep in mind that The Seven Universal Laws always remain in perfect harmony. The first three laws are constant, meaning they are absolute and can never be changed; they have always existed and will always exist. The last four laws are transitory, meaning that they can be applied better to create your ideal reality. I am not implying that you should ignore the last four laws, since they still govern the universe. With that said, I have included The Seven Universal Laws just as they appear in The Kybalion.

The Seven Universal Laws
THE SEVEN HERMETIC PRINCIPLES

"The Principles of Truth are Seven; he who knows these, understandingly, possesses the Magic Key before whose touch all the Doors of the Temple fly open." — The Kybalion.

The Seven Hermetic Principles, upon which the entire Hermetic Philosophy is based, are as follows:

I. The Principle of Mentalism.
II. The Principle of Correspondence.
III. The Principle of Vibration.
IV. The Principle of Polarity.
V. The Principle of Rhythm.
VI. The Principle of Cause and Effect.
VII. The Principle of Gender.

I. THE PRINCIPLE OF MENTALISM.
"THE ALL is MIND; The Universe is Mental." — The Kybalion.

This Principle embodies the truth that "All is Mind." It explains that THE ALL (which is the Substantial Reality underlying all the outward manifestations and appearances which we know under the terms of "The Material Universe"; the "Phenomena of Life"; "Matter"; "Energy"; and in short, all that is apparent to our material senses) is SPIRIT, which in itself is UNKNOWABLE and UNDEFINABLE, but which may be considered and thought of as AN UNIVERSAL, INFINITE, LIVING MIND. It also explains that all the phenomenal world or universe is simply a Mental Creation of THE ALL, subject to the Laws of Created Things and that the universe, as a whole, and in its parts or units, has its existence in the Mind of THE ALL, in which Mind we "live and move and have our being." This Principle, by establishing the Mental Nature of the Universe, easily explains all of the varied mental and psychic phenomena that occupy such a large portion of the public attention and which, without such explanation, are non-understandable and defy scientific treatment. An understanding of this great Hermetic Principle of Mentalism enables the individual to readily grasp the laws of the Mental Universe, and to apply the same to his well-being and advancement. The Hermetic Student is enabled to apply intelligently the great Mental Laws, instead of using them in a haphazard manner. With the Master-Key in his possession, the student may unlock the many doors of the mental and psychic temple of knowledge and enter the same freely and intelligently. This Principle explains the true nature of "Energy," "Power," and "Matter," and why and how all these are subordinate to the Mastery of Mind. One of the old Hermetic Masters wrote, long ages ago: "He who grasps the truth of the Mental Nature of the Universe is well advanced on The Path to Mastery." These words are as true today as at the time they were first written. Without this Master-Key, Mastery is impossible, and the student knocks in vain at the many doors of The Temple.

II. THE PRINCIPLE OF CORRESPONDENCE.
"As above, so below; as below, so above." –The Kybalion

This Principle embodies the truth that there is always a Correspondence between the laws and phenomena of the various planes of Being and Life. The old Hermetic axiom ran in these words: "As above, so below; as below, so above." The grasping of this Principle gives one the means of solving many a dark paradox, and hidden secret of Nature. There are planes beyond our knowing, but when we apply the Principle of Correspondence to them we are able to understand much that would otherwise be unknowable to us. This Principle is of universal application and manifestation, on the various planes of the material, mental, and spiritual universe–it is an Universal Law. The ancient

Hermetists considered this Principle as one of the most important mental instruments by which man was able to pry aside the obstacles which hid from view the Unknown. Its use even tore aside the Veil of Isis to the extent that a glimpse of the face of the goddess might be caught. Just as a knowledge of the Principles of Geometry enables man to measure distant suns and their movements, while seated in his observatory, so a knowledge of the Principle of Correspondence enables Man to reason intelligently from the Known to the Unknown. Studying the monad, he understands the archangel.

III. THE PRINCIPLE OF VIBRATION.
"Nothing rests; everything moves; everything vibrates."
–The Kybalion.

This Principle embodies the truth that "everything is in motion"; "everything vibrates"; "nothing is at rest"; facts which Modern Science endorses, and which each new scientific discovery tends to verify. And yet this Hermetic Principle was enunciated thousands of years ago by the Masters of Ancient Egypt. This Principle explains that the differences between different manifestations of Matter, Energy, Mind, and even Spirit, result largely from varying rates of Vibration. From THE ALL, which is Pure Spirit, down to the grossest form of Matter, all is in vibration–the higher the vibration, the higher the position in the scale. The vibration of Spirit is at such an infinite rate of intensity and rapidity that it is practically at rest–just as a rapidly moving wheel seems to be motionless. At the other end of the scale, there are gross forms of matter whose vibrations are so low as to seem at rest. Between these poles, there are millions upon millions of varying degrees of vibration. From corpuscle and electron, atom and molecule, to worlds and universes, everything is in vibratory motion. This is also true on the planes of energy and force (which are but varying degrees of vibration); and also on the mental planes (whose states depend upon vibrations); and even on to the spiritual planes. An understanding of this Principle, with the appropriate formulas, enables Hermetic students to control their own mental vibrations as well as those of others. The Masters also apply this Principle to the conquering of Natural phenomena, in various ways. "He who understands the Principle of Vibration, has grasped the sceptre of power," says one of the old writers.

IV. THE PRINCIPLE OF POLARITY.

"Everything is Dual; everything has poles; everything has its pair of opposites; like and unlike are the same; opposites are identical in nature, but different in degree; extremes meet; all truths are but half-truths; all paradoxes may be reconciled."
 –The Kybalion.

This Principle embodies the truth that "everything is dual"; "everything has two poles"; "everything has its pair of opposites," all of which were old Hermetic axioms. It explains the old paradoxes, that have perplexed so many, which have been stated as follows: "Thesis and antithesis are identical in nature, but different in degree"; "opposites are the same, differing only in degree"; "the pairs of opposites may be reconciled"; "extremes meet"; "everything is and isn't, at the same time"; "all truths are but half-truths"; "every truth is half-false"; "there are two sides to everything," etc., etc., etc. It explains that in everything there are two poles, or opposite aspects, and that "opposites" are really only the two extremes of the same thing, with many varying degrees between them. To illustrate: Heat and Cold, although "opposites," are really the same thing, the differences consisting merely of degrees of the same thing. Look at your thermometer and see if you can discover where "heat" terminates and "cold" begins! There is no such thing as "absolute heat" or "absolute cold"--the two terms "heat" and "cold" simply indicate varying degrees of the same thing, and that "same thing" which manifests as "heat" and "cold" is merely a form, variety, and rate of Vibration. So "heat" and "cold" are simply the "two poles" of that which we call "Heat"--and the phenomena attendant thereupon are manifestations of the Principle of Polarity. The same Principle manifests in the case of "Light and Darkness," which are the same thing, the difference consisting of varying degrees between the two poles of the phenomena. Where does "darkness" leave off, and "light" begin? What is the difference between "Large and Small"? Between "Hard and Soft"? Between "Black and White"? Between "Sharp and Dull"? Between "Noise and Quiet"? Between "High and Low"? Between "Positive and Negative"? The Principle of Polarity explains these paradoxes and no other Principle can supersede it. The same Principle operates on the Mental Plane. Let us take a radical and extreme example--that of "Love and Hate," two mental states apparently totally different. And yet there are degrees of Hate and degrees of Love, and a middle point in which we use the terms "Like or Dislike," which shade into each other so gradually that sometimes we are at a loss to know whether we "like" or "dislike" or "neither." And all are simply degrees of the same thing, as you will see if you will but think a moment. And, more than this (and considered of more importance by the Hermetists), it is possible to change the vibrations of Hate to the vibrations of Love, in one's own mind and in the minds of others. Many of you, who read these lines, have had personal experiences of the involuntary rapid transition from Love to Hate and the reverse, in your own case and that of others. And you will therefore realize the possibility of this being accomplished by the use of the Will, by means of the Hermetic formulas. "Good and Evil" are but the poles of the same thing and the Hermetist understands the art of transmuting Evil into Good, by means of an application of the Principle of Polarity. In short, the "Art of Polarization" becomes a phase of "Mental Alchemy" known and practiced by the ancient and modern Hermetic Masters. An understanding of the Principle will enable one to change his own Polarity, as well as that of others, if he will devote the time and study necessary to master the art.

V. THE PRINCIPLE OF RHYTHM.

"Everything flows, out and in; everything has its tides; all things rise and fall; the pendulum-swing manifests in everything; the measure of the swing to the right is the measure of the swing to the left; rhythm compensates."
– *The Kybalion.*

This Principle embodies the truth that in everything there is manifested a measured motion, to and fro; a flow and inflow; a swing backward and forward; a pendulum-like movement; a tide-like ebb and flow; a high-tide and low-tide; between the two poles which exist in accordance with the Principle of Polarity described a moment ago. There is always an action and a reaction; an advance and a retreat; a rising and a sinking. This is in the affairs of the Universe, suns, worlds, men, animals, mind, energy, and matter. This law is manifest in the creation and destruction of worlds; in the rise and fall of nations; in the life of all things; and finally in the mental states of Man (and it is with this latter that the Hermetists find the understanding of the Principle most important). The Hermetists have grasped this Principle, finding its universal application, and have also discovered certain means to overcome its effects in themselves by the use of the appropriate formulas and methods. They apply the Mental Law of Neutralization. They cannot annul the Principle, or cause it to cease its operation, but they have learned how to escape its effects upon themselves to a certain degree depending upon the Mastery of the Principle. They have learned how to USE it, instead of being USED BY it. In this and similar methods, consist the Art of the Hermetists. The Master of Hermetics polarizes himself at the point at which he desires to rest and then neutralizes the Rhythmic swing of the pendulum which would tend to carry him to the other pole. All individuals who have attained any degree of Self-Mastery do this to a certain degree, more or less unconsciously, but the Master does this consciously, and by the use of his Will, and attains a degree of Poise and Mental Firmness almost impossible of belief on the part of the masses who are swung backward and forward like a pendulum. This Principle and that of Polarity have been closely studied by the Hermetists, and the methods of counteracting, neutralizing, and USING them form an important part of the Hermetic Mental Alchemy.

VI. THE PRINCIPLE OF CAUSE AND EFFECT.

"Every Cause has its Effect; every Effect has its Cause; everything happens according to Law; Chance is but a name for Law not recognized; there are many planes of causation, but nothing escapes the Law." – The Kybalion.

This Principle embodies the fact that there is a Cause for every Effect; an Effect from every Cause. It explains that: "Everything Happens according to Law"; that nothing ever "merely happens"; that there is no such thing as Chance; that while there are various planes of Cause and Effect, the higher dominating the lower planes, still nothing ever entirely escapes the Law. The Hermetists understand the art and methods of rising above the ordinary plane of Cause and Effect, to a certain degree and by mentally rising to a higher plane they become Causers instead of Effects. The masses of people are carried along, obedient to environment; the wills and desires of others stronger than themselves; heredity; suggestion; and other outward causes moving them about like pawns on the Chessboard of Life. But the Masters, rising to the plane above, dominate their moods, characters, qualities, and powers, as well as the environment surrounding them, and become Movers instead of pawns. They help to PLAY THE GAME OF LIFE, instead of being played and moved about by other wills and environment. They USE the Principle instead of being its tools. The Masters obey the Causation of the higher planes, but they help to RULE on their own plane. In this statement there is condensed a wealth of Hermetic knowledge–let him read who can.

VII. THE PRINCIPLE OF GENDER.
"Gender is in everything; everything has its Masculine and Feminine Principles; Gender manifests on all planes."
–The Kybalion.

This Principle embodies the truth that there is GENDER manifested in everything–the Masculine and Feminine Principles ever at work. This is true not only of the Physical Plane, but of the Mental and even the Spiritual Planes. On the Physical Plane, the Principle manifests as SEX, on the higher planes it takes higher forms, but the Principle is ever the same. No creation, physical, mental or spiritual, is possible without this Principle. An understanding of its laws will throw light on many a subject that has perplexed the minds of men. The Principle of Gender works ever in the direction of generation, regeneration, and creation. Everything, and every person, contains the two Elements or Principles, or this great Principle, within it, him or her. Every Male thing has the Female Element also; every Female contains also the Male Principle. If you would understand the philosophy of Mental and Spiritual Creation, Generation, and Re-generation, you must understand and study this Hermetic Principle. It contains the solution of many mysteries of Life. We caution you that this Principle has no reference to the many base, pernicious and degrading lustful theories, teachings and practices, which are taught under fanciful titles, and which are a prostitution of the great natural principle of Gender. Such base revivals of the ancient infamous forms of Phallicism tend to ruin mind, body and soul, and the Hermetic Philosophy has ever sounded the warning note against these degraded teachings which tend toward lust, licentiousness, and perversion of Nature's principles. If you seek such teachings, you must go elsewhere for them–Hermeticism contains nothing for you

The Seven Universal Laws

along these lines. To the pure, all things are pure; to the base, all things are base.

❧

As I stated before, a number of other books have been written about these seven laws or principles, using somewhat more modern language, but the Kybalion is the original. The moment you consciously comprehend these principles you can create whatever you desire in your life. Take the time to understand the wisdom on the pages in this small but remarkable book. It will spiritually empower you.

---

* The Kybalion is based upon ancient Hermetic (Hermes Trismegistus) philosophy that has been passed down through the centuries, The Kybalion was originally published anonymously in the early 1900's (by Three Initiates).

The Cycle Of Life

"Man appears for a little while to laugh and weep, to work and play, and then to go to make room for those who shall follow him in the never-ending cycle."
- Aiden Wilson Tozer

You probably are aware that everything in this universe is subject to a Cycle of Life. An atom, an ant, a human, the tide, the seasons, the moon, the earth, the solar system, the milky way, the universe; everything has a Cycle of Life. Everything known to humans is energy so everything falls under this principle, law or cycle, whatever we decide to call it.

For us humans the cycle is very clear: we are born, we grow up; we reproduce, we mature and we pass away. However, to a certain degree human beings have control of their existence; we still are subject to this Cycle of Life but we possess the ability to choose, we have free will. Sadly a large number of the population choose to behave thoughtlessly; constantly making the wrong choices in life. Everyone has to make decisions on a daily basis; the grocery store manager, the yoga teacher, the student in 7th grade; any decision we make determines our destiny.

Have you ever heard the old saying, there is a time and place for everything? What this old quote implies is the fact that there are periods or moments (cycles) in your life when making the right choices will lead to absolute success; on the other hand if you make the same choice during a different moment, the outcome is not as favourable as you expected; the Cycle of Life is the reason for this distinctiveness at the end result; many people ignore or don't understand the principle of the Cycle of Life. However, if you take the time to learn it and apply it to your life both your personal and professional life will improve tremendously.

From Freud to Piaget and Erikson, they all agree that the human life can be divided into stages (cycles); however, they disagree on how these stages are divided. The principle of the Cycle of Life is based on the concept that the human life is divided into cycles of seven years each; these cycles influence our life in every aspect: emotionally, psychologically, and physically. I

The Cycle Of Life

will not pretend to be a doctor in medicine or psychiatrist to go into full detail about the physical or mental development in every stage, so I will touch very briefly on the developments we experience in every cycle.

Of course the first cycle is from birth to age seven; in the first cycle we go through an incredible process of learning. It is during this time that we develop a very basic response to truth, which later becomes our moral codes. Our imagination is more vivid than any other time in our life. Apparently our greatest strengths and fears originate from this cycle.

The second cycle is from age seven to age fourteen; we continue to grow in every aspect; emotionally we keep developing more complex skills and by the age of twelve to thirteen we leap into puberty and adolescence.

The third cycle is from age fourteen to age twenty-one; many believe that this is the most important cycle of them all. It is during this cycle where we become self conscious; our "grown-up" personality begins to take shape, a new found appreciation for art, music, past times and people expand even further. In most countries the age at which a person is considered an adult is at age eighteen.

The fourth cycle is from age twenty-one to twenty-eight; this cycle is where most people emotionally and mentally enter into adulthood. It is during this period that we lay the foundation of our career, relationships, and personal boundaries.

The fifth cycle is from age twenty-eight to thirty-five; during this period we achieve top physical condition. Strength and reproductive capacity are at their peak. It is during this cycle where most people expect to have accomplished important milestones like finding a partner, having a first child and buying a home. Reaching certain levels of stability with the ambition of more success ahead makes this period a crucial stepping stone for the next cycle.

The sixth cycle is from age thirty-five to forty-two; this cycle is the first half of what is considered middle age. We start to notice some physical changes; our metabolism slows down, loss of muscle mass and tone. Psychologically we develop a better balance between career and family.

The seventh cycle is from age forty-two to forty-nine; this cycle is the second half of what is considered middle age. Physical changes continue to develop; hair starts to turn gray, increasing wrinkles, and decline in hearing and sight. During this period many people want to make a mark in the world so they change their life directions. In many cases mental stress sets in due to caring for ageing parents or other family members.

The eighth cycle is from age forty-nine to fifty-six; something very interesting happens during this cycle. The apparent physical decline forces a person to pay attention inwards instead of outwards; for many a new sense of spiritual awakening begins. For this reason the majority of people find a greater enjoyment in life during this time.

The ninth cycle is from age fifty-six to sixty-three; This period is considered a time for winding down; for most it is a time for final adjustment before retirement age. We become more health conscious since health risks such as heart disease increases. Studies also shows memory decreases starting in the late fifties, if we do not exercise our brain.

The tenth cycle is from age sixty-three to seventy; This cycle is what many consider "A New Beginning." During this time your creativity goes into high gear; you have an urge to express yourself. A higher sense of detachment from material things begins to take hold.

Keep in mind that every human life is unique and it is true that the Cycle of Life is always influencing your life; however, nothing is set in stone. Every cycle promotes new benefits and challenges; life experiences are up to you to create so don't hold back, live every day with joy and passion. Gandhi expressed this better than anyone else could when he quoted *"Live as if you were to die tomorrow. Learn as if you were to live forever."* Always concentrate on the present and plan for the future; there is no point in thinking about unpleasant things that already happened. Instead tend to things on which you can take action.

It is essential that you create your own opportunities at the right time; don't wait for others to do it for you, take action. Set your short and long term goals in life; it is up to you to design your ideal life. Every major corporation around the world has a business plan, so should you; make your 1 year, 3 year, 5 year and 10 year plan.

Now that you're aware that our lives are divided in cycles of seven years each, let me share with you the following: every year of your life is also divided in seven cycles. In the following exercise you can figure out in which cycle of the year you are presently in. By having the advantage of knowing in which cycle you are presently, you will be able to excel in all your projects and avoid misfortunes or unpleasant surprises. It is very important that you understand that the conventional calender has nothing to do with the yearly Cycle of Life. This is your own personal yearly cycle. It begins from the day of your birthday and extends to one day before your next birthday.

*Calender is based upon the ancient and esoteric science.

Yearly Cycle

Step 1.

Take a calender and starting with your birthday, count fifty-two days. This is your first cycle; continue to count every fifty-two days to make a record for the entire year; this way you will be able to tell in which cycle you are in.

First Cycle

Date _____ to _____

This cycle is about new beginnings. Your first cycle always begins with a strong momentum to start new ventures or build on past accomplishments while avoiding obstacles. During this time you will create great opportunities to grow personally and professionally. This is the best time for you to invest in every aspect of your life: health, relationships, finances, etc. There is no better time to take action than during this cycle.

Second Cycle

Date _____ to _____

"What you plant is what you reap." You will see the signs of growth around your projects; you will start to notice new patterns as your initial investment continue to develop. This active growth phase will continues as long as you pay close attention to all your affairs. It is best to avoid starting new long term projects, juggling too many projects at once will lead to failure in business and turmoil in your personal life. There is no better time to get yourself organized than during this cycle; throwing away the unwanted and old stuff, will allow you to create more room for new things.

Third Cycle

Date _____ to _____

    During this cycle it is essential to stay positive. This is the time to invest in yourself; time to spend more time with people who are compatible with you, people who are successful, overachievers and positive for your growth; hire a mentor or a coach, someone who will work with you to help you achieve your goals. Your projects you started or build upon in your first cycle should be well-balanced and already bearing profits, at the personal and professional level.

Fourth Cycle

Date _____ to _____

It is time to review your life and prioritize. Keep in mind that a balanced and a meaningful life is possible only if you can achieve harmony in every aspect of your life. Generally there is an atmosphere of worry during this cycle. This is when you seriously start perceiving the effects of the actions you took in earlier cycles. This is also a great time to ask for feedback regarding personal and business affairs; approach colleagues, boss, or an advisor since they will give their feedback objectively.

Fifth Cycle

Date _____ to _____

    No matter what your field is, during this cycle you will experience a great amount of success in your business. This is the period to embrace change; move forward on those previous matters that seemed risky; the bigger your risks, the bigger your return. Strive to be #1 in what you do. By all means, avoid procrastinating during this cycle, since this is the last cycle of growth in your personal year. There is no better time to get out of your comfort zone and try new things.

Sixth Cycle

Date _____ to _____

Things will start to settle down in business/work; not particularly in any negative matter but this is the perfect time to step back and allow your business/work to keep running its course. It's a great time to achieve peace and relaxation, to socialize and connect with old friends; work on making deeper connections. Excellent opportunity to travel or to go on vacation; perfect time to remove any external pressure and let go of any stress or unwanted baggage. Stay away from any dishonest characters or business proposals.

Seventh Cycle

Date _____ to _____

You have to be very careful in your affairs during your last cycle. This is when things could go in the wrong direction or even completely fall apart; there is no reason to fear this period, remember that this cycle is part of the Cycle of Life. You could say this is the cycle of "letting go." Letting go of anything that was holding you back. It is during this period you can look back and contemplate all the successes and mistakes you experienced during your whole yearly cycle; always remember to embrace both success and mistakes since you learn from both experiences. During this time it is most prudent to plan well before taking any action; in fact it is most advisable to delay any new enterprise until the new yearly cycle begins.

Step 2.

Keep a copy of your yearly cycle on hands at all time so you can refer to it when you need it.

Step 3.

Share the knowledge with family, friends and colleagues.

Light At The End Of The Tunnel

"There was a beautiful and bright light at the end of the tunnel, I felt so peaceful that I no longer fear death."
- Angela Wallace

Just about everyone nowadays either knows or has heard of someone that has experienced NDE (Near-death experience), maybe even you the reader had this amazing experience. These phenomena are usually reported after the person has been pronounced clinically dead or otherwise very close to death, therefore the term Near-death experience. With the incredible advancement in medicine and the developments in cardiac resuscitation techniques, the number of reported NDEs has increased exponentially.

Most individuals share the same description during a NDE: passing into or through a tunnel, floating towards a bright light, out-of-body experience, awareness of past events in his or her life, unearthly lights, peacefulness, joy, and encounters with mystical entities or deceased relatives. What is amazing is the fact that studies have found no association between NDEs and gender, age, level of education, religious beliefs, ethnicity, or even the location. The truth is that reports of NDEs in people who suffer life-threatening illness or traumas are unexplained by current science.

Like many people around the world, I also have a NDE story to share. This is the true story that transformed the life of two people, my father (Jose Incer Sr.) and I. The lesson that I learned from this experience became deeply ingrained in my psyche, more than any lesson that I learned in school or from any book.

It was in June of 2003, my father was living in Teustepe (Teustepe is a municipality in Boaco, Nicaragua). I was living in Plantation, Florida at the time. We spoke over the phone once in a while, to keep in touch. He was a man of few words when it came to the phone. But in the middle of June of 2004. I made a very important call, in fact it was the last time my father would speak to me, I just didn't know it at the time. I made that call the night before he had to undergo a critical operation to remove a malignant tumor from his throat that was starting to obstruct his airway. This was one of many complications that my father was dealing with at the time. We spoke briefly about how we felt about each other, then I wished him good luck. I told him I would call him as soon as he arrived back to my aunt's house (my father stayed with my aunt whenever he stayed in Managua, the capital of Nicaragua).

The surgeons were successful removing the tumor but unfortunately my father lost his voice permanently. We could no longer communicate over the phone. After speaking with family members I decided to wait for a couple of months until my father fully recuperated from the operation. By August he was back to his old self, so I was told. So I took a week off from work and flew down to Nicaragua.

My cousin and my father were already waiting for me by the time I arrived at the airport. I was anxious to see him, I did not know what to expect. I made my way through customs and arrived at the terminal; there, I saw both my father and my cousin, my father looked great, he seemed like a different man; I was so happy to see him doing so well; I hugged him and he gave me a big smile. I grabbed my bags and started walking toward the exit. I kept looking at him and noticed there was something different about him. At the time I could not put my finger on it but there was definitely something different about him.

After a short drive we arrived at my aunt's house. There was a small family gathering waiting for us. We all talked for a while, then everyone went about their daily business. A couple of days passed and there were a few more family gatherings everyday, but one afternoon I found myself watching TV all alone in the living room, the only other person in the house was my father and he was in his room. It was getting dark, I didn't hear when he approached, next thing I knew I felt a tap on my left shoulder, my father was standing next to me. With a hand gesture, he asked me to follow him to his room and asked me to sit down on his bed and to pay close attention to what he had to communicate to me. With body gestures and writing, he stated something that I could not have anticipated. He told me that during the operation he passed-away. I was shocked and remained silent. Nothing could have prepared me for what followed.

He told me that he clearly remembered laying down in the operating room. All of the sudden he found himself in a peaceful prairie with green rolling hills all around him, not a single person as far as he could see. The warm sun was high in the blue sky. He remembered feeling a warm breeze brushing against his face that felt so comforting. He told me he felt confused because he couldn't remember how he got to this place, where ever that place was. He expressed that he could sense and feel everything just like normal. He stood there for a while trying to figure out what was going on. Slowly he started to walk trying to reach the top of one the hill and as he reached the top, all he could see were more green hills all around. He started to run, he reached the top of the next hill and then next, and the next.

At one point he stopped, he kept asking himself "how did I get here?" He told me he started to feel disheartened. At that moment he felt someone tap his shoulder, it startled him. He told me he saw a man standing next to him. He was tall, white with long blond hair, fair skin and blue eyes. My father told me this man standing next to him looked like a rock star he used to admire when he was younger. He told me that he felt this being was peaceful and caring, he felt so calm standing next to this tall man. My father was facing this being, fascinated by his presence. With a simple gesture of extending his arm, the man asked my father to turn around. As he turned around, right in front of them there was a huge mountain where just seconds before there were only green hills.

Light At The End Of The Tunnel

My father immediately noticed that there were two big caves at the bottom of the mountain, and the man that was standing next to him was also standing next to each of the entrances of the caves, but in one entrance he was wearing a white robe and in the other entrance he was wearing a black robe. My father told me he was confused, he could not understand what was going on. Then the tall being next to him extended his arm again, and my father heard a voice in his head asking him to choose one of the caves. My father told me he didn't know what to do. Then all of the sudden he felt a sense not go into any of the caves.

My father turned around and started to run, he ran as fast as he could, hill after hill. As he reached the top of one of those hills, out in the distance he saw his own body in gigantic dimension laying on the ground, he recalled rushing toward it and leaping into it. He told me that's when he felt coming back into his own body. The next thing he remembered was waking up in the recovery room.

This experience that he described took me completely by surprise. You see my father had been a devout atheist all his life, a none believer in the spiritual life. All my life I knew my father as a well educated man that spoke frankly when he was serious about a subject; so I had no doubt about his sincerity.

It took me some time to make sense of what happened that night. But finally, I realized that I was right about the feeling I had that day when he picked me up at the airport, there was definitely something different about him. That experience had changed him, he was a different man. I know that event changed my father's life and eventually it also changed my life.

My father passed away not to long after that experience. But I know now that he is in a better place, because he returned to that peaceful prairie and I know that he made the right choice.

Calling on a Guide

Step 1.

Find a place where you will not be disturbed for about 30 minutes. Sit in a straight back chair. Close your eyes and take three deep easy breaths to relax yourself. Continue to relax, breathing easily and naturally.

Step 2.

Imagine you are moving forward in a long hallway. The hallway can look like anything you want. Notice there are doors all along this hallway. Each door will take you to a special place or event where you will meet only Guides and Highly evolved entities who mean you well.

Step 3.

Count to seven, and imagine yourself standing in front of one these doors. Notice all the details of the place you are standing, the more details the better. Put your hand on the door knob. Open the door, step through the door. Take a few minutes to pay close attention to all the details, sounds, and sensations. Concentrate on this new environment.

Step 4.

Wherever you are, find a comfortable place to sit down. Focus on the feeling of relaxation, free from distractions or any emotional obstacle that prevent you from encountering your Guide.

Step 5.

Notice that your Guide begins to move toward you. See her/him, feel her/him, hear her/him. You can feel your Guide moving closer and closer. Sense her/his presence.

Step 6.

Begin to have a conversation with your guide. Feel free to ask for advise or answers you are searching for. When you are done with the conversation, thank your Guide for giving you advise and answering your questions.

Step 7.

Imagine getting up and walking back to the door. Count to three and open your eyes. You will feel wide awake, refreshed, and very positive about what you have just experienced.

Part Seven
Conclusion

Keep Moving Forward

"You are always a student, never a master.
You have to keep moving forward."
- Conrad Hall

Always keep in mind that you have the last word on how well you do in your personal and professional life. By putting into practice the knowledge you have acquired by reading the pages of this book you can take control of the way you think, feel, and act. It is my hope that the information that I have shared will guide you along the right path to success.

You might not realize it but if you are in search of genuine self-improvement; you are already on a state of growth. Remember that growth is a process not a destination; so always continue to invest in yourself by learning, practicing, and sharing your wisdom with others.

I'm well aware that it is normal to get tired of working on self-improvement all the time; but let's be honest, if you don't take care of yourself, who will? No one has more interest in you than yourself. I know that if you have read this far into the this book you truly want to empower your life.

Today is the moment of truth, the past is behind you and the future is up for grabs; given the proven power of the techniques and exercises that you have learned; you must start now, why wait? Too often, we find ourselves waiting for the "perfect time," just to find out that perfect timing doesn't exist; if there was such a thing as the perfect time, then I will have to say that the perfect time is now.

As you keep moving forward in your own personal journey don't allow anyone to deter you from your goals. Prevent any negative suggestions from taking root in your mind. If someone tells you that you cannot expect to be like Dorothy Hodgkin, Dian Fossey, Steve Jobs, or Mark Twain; thank them for their opinion and ignore their words. Because yes, you can become an inspirational person who can change the world; in fact, I truly hope so. Even that we probably have never met, I

Keep Moving Forward

am 100% behind you. Don't settle for anything but to be the best, aim for the gold. I want you to always keep the following though in your heart *"The universe created me for a purpose; I am here and my life has a special meaning."*

Share The Knowledge

"If you have knowledge, let others light their candles in it."
- Margaret Fuller

Share The Knowledge

I wrote this book for you, I sincerely hope that it will transform your life into an amazing journey.

If you found the information in this book useful; respectfully I will ask you to recommend it to other people. You can be part of this growing movement by informing your family, friends, coworkers and the public in general about it. So now I am asking you to take action and please help me spread the word of self-empowerment and higher consciousness.

You can post messages about the this book and its content in Facebook, Twitter, LinkedIn or any other social networking site; you can email your friends. If you have contact in the media; tell them about it, they might get an interesting article or story out of it. If you are in a book club you can recommend it.

You can post a brilliant review on Amazon, Barnes & Noble or Half.com.

If you need help on your journey, or need some questions answered. I am easily contacted by email or phone. I'll be happy to hear from you.

To your success,

Jose Incer C Ht, CPLC, NLP, CPT
www.joseincer.com
www.nautiluslife.com
jincer@nautiluslife.com
954-381-9632

"In the end, it's not the years in your life that count.
It's the life in your years."
- Abraham Lincoln